LEARNING TO PARENT
IN THE LIGHT
IN A DARK WORLD

MY JOURNEY OF SORROW AND JOY

*To Kathryn
With Love —
Karen Sue Smith*

KAREN SUE SMITH

DEDICATION

"Fixing our eyes on Jesus, the author and perfecter of faith."
Hebrews 12:2

This book is dedicated to my Lord and Savior Jesus Christ, who has saved me, delivered me and walks with me every day! My heart longs to continue to draw closer to You!

"so that you may become blameless and pure, "children of God without fault in a warped and crooked generation." Then you will shine among them like stars in the sky." Philippians 2:15

This book is also dedicated to Dwight, Hudson, Sara, Hannah, Jessie, Jonathan and Arron. I thank God for each of your precious lives who bring so much light into mine.

ACKNOWLEDGMENTS

I want to honor those who have sacrificed so much on my behalf in praying and caring for me and our family. You are a treasure and have helped me know God and His love!

Also, my heart overflows with gratefulness for all of my precious friends and family who helped me in the writing and editing process! Your corrections and insights made this book what it is today. A special thanks to my husband and best friend Dwight for his hours of listening and editing of the manuscript.

TABLE OF CONTENTS

CHAPTER 1 OUR JOURNEY BEGINS

As I take up my pen to write my story, we are in the middle of a cold Chicago winter, where the mercury dips below zero and the wind chills are extremely dangerous! As I write rning the temperature is -9°F. But this opening story is not about the weather, it is about our furnace. We have lived in our house here in Wheaton for over fifteen years, and our furnace has faithfully brought us through these bitter winters. However, we know that our furnace is getting along in years, and during the extreme cold needs to be nurtured along. It is not easy putting in all the long hours of heating our house!

What happens to you when you face harsh weather in your life? Do you feel fragile? Do you need extra care? What do you do when losses, trauma or hardship visit your life? What do you do when you don't know how to move forward because you are overwhelmed?

These are questions that we all must face at some point, because we live in a world that is broken and in need of repair. Jesus said, "*In this world you will have trouble, but take heart for I have overcome the world!*" (John 16:33).

One thing I notice on these bitterly cold days is that often, along with the cold, we have brilliant blue skies. With no clouds covering the sun the snow sparkles in its light!

What will be my focus on these days? Will I focus on the bitter cold, or the brilliant sun?

Dear reader, you are about to enter my journey of how I learned to live and parent in the light when my world was full of darkness.

I pray that as you read the lessons that God taught me about dealing with loss, treasuring life, and parenting, you will find hope and light in your own areas of darkness. I also pray that the lessons I learned will be a blessing to you, as they have been to me.

OUR STORY BEGINS

There are moments in life where we are transformed, and the direction of our life is changed.

All of these defining moments happen in the context of a story.

This is the reason why I would like to invite you into the story of my three children who are no longer here on earth. Although their lives on earth were but a breath, each child's life brought me into a defining moment that would not only bring transformation, but would leave a mark on my life, changing the way I lived!

Why am I so passionate about children, and helping them grow in their relationships with God and their families?

Why do I want to provide families with resources, so they can make the most of this season of their lives?

I am passionate because I know what a treasure each child is.

I know how quickly children grow up, so I know how important it is to make every moment count!

- How do you parent your children with purpose, making the present moment the best it can be?
- How do you raise a child in our current culture, in a time when we have more voices than ever calling for our attention?
- How do you parent kids who have 24/7 access to the Internet and emerging new technologies?
- How do you care for them when they are daily exposed to a dark world?

- How do we nurture our children to grow up connected to God and their family?

These are important questions to answer as we love the children around us!

As we have walked the journey of being parents, God has given us keys of how to parent in the light in a dark world. This path has been full of overwhelming sorrow, but also more joy than a heart can contain. I invite you into our story not only to learn the keys that God gave us, but also to see that God is faithful and will never leave us or forsake us!

OUR LOVE STORY

It was my second year working at the name tag table at the annual Campus Crusade for Christ Christmas Conference. I loved being able to greet the students as they arrived. There is always a lot of excitement at the beginning of an event, and this year's conference was no exception. As the stream of students began to thin, there was one more visitor to my table. Noting his ripped sweater, I politely answered his questions. His name was Dwight. He was also on staff, but was not working at the conference. I commented to myself that he did not seem to be the typical Campus Crusade staff member.

Later I saw Dwight again at a book table outside of the main meeting room. It was there we discovered a mutual love for God, and for learning and listening to what God was saying. He invited me to lunch, and I accepted his invitation.

Being on staff was a wonderful experience, full of travel and constantly meeting new friends. So I did not think much about this lunch date. I had resolved in my heart to only date someone if he lived where I worked, in Muncie, Indiana. He lived five and a half hours away in Michigan, therefore he did not fall into my criteria. After a nice lunch I thanked him for our time together and wished him well in his new staff assignment.

But that was not an acceptable answer to him. I could see in Dwight's face a questioning of why I even spoke those words! We continued to talk here and there for the remainder of the conference, and then the calls and weekend visits started after the event was over. This all turned into a whirlwind romance. We were engaged in five weeks, and married within six months! Now, twenty-eight years later I still thank God every day for my best friend, and the love of my life!

We have journeyed together through both very good and very difficult times, but he is still to me the most wonderful man in the world!

CHAPTER 2 HUDSON'S LIFE

Our first six years of marriage were full of ministry, adventure, and travel. Being on staff with Campus Crusade brought us to interesting places and connected us with amazing people. We lived in Indiana and Georgia. Then God called us to leave the staff of Campus Crusade, so we spent a transition year in New York before finally landing in Massachusetts. Dwight found his niche working with computers, and I began working on my Master of Divinity degree at Gordon Conwell Theological Seminary. It was two years into the program that I discovered I was pregnant with our first child.

Living in the seminary apartments, we were surrounded by families with young children, so it seemed natural for us to join their ranks with children of our own.

When we found out I was pregnant we had all the normal reactions of joy, anticipation and hope! I did well the first three months of our new baby's life. We enjoyed the sound of hearing our baby's heartbeat for the first time. I gave in to cravings for food, and looked for extra minutes to rest between my studies.

On September 11, 1996 we were to have our 18-week ultrasound as part of our routine prenatal care. We were both looking forward to seeing our baby, and if possible to find out if we were having a girl or a boy.

At the ultrasound we received the good news that I was carrying a boy! We named him Hudson Taylor, after James Hudson Taylor, who had founded the China Inland Mission. James Hudson Taylor's life had influenced both of us, encouraging us to pursue God and pray for those who needed Christ.

I remember well the day after the ultrasound. Dwight was working in Boston, and I was at the computer, researching and writing. The phone rang. When I answered, the voice on the other end of the line was my doctor. At first, I was confused. Why was he calling me now? Then my heart sank as he told me that the ultrasound showed that my baby would not live! I was stunned, but my first question was, "Can the baby survive inside of me?" He said we could talk about the details later. My next step was to go to Boston for a level-two ultrasound to confirm the diagnosis. I hung up the phone in disbelief.

The words only began to sink in after the call ended. My friend across the hall was home, and she not only cried with me, but helped me pick up Dwight from the train. Thoughts raced through our minds. Maybe the doctor was wrong? Maybe everything was fine?

Friends from our church came over that evening to spend time in prayer with us. We prayed for Hudson. They anointed us with oil. This prayer time was only the beginning of the prayers that we would pray, as we would find out later. Throughout Hudson's life, God would call us and others to fervent, consistent, believing prayer, first on Hudson's behalf and then on mine!

I awoke the next morning, still hoping that maybe this was all a mistake, and I could go back to my daily routine of studying and enjoying the new life inside of me. Our friends Peter and Lupe said they would drive us to the appointment in Boston. Before we left we again spent time in prayer. During this prayer time Lupe saw a vision of a beautiful purple mum with a yellow center. She explained to me that mums are a strong and healthy plant, even through the sometimes-harsh weather of fall.

I was so thankful that Dwight and I had the company of friends for this trip into Boston! When we arrived at the building where the ultrasound would take place, we took the elevator up to the testing floor. As we stepped out into the hallway my eyes were immediately drawn to several large pots filled with purple and yellow mums! Their beautiful petals brought comfort to my racing heart and mind. God was with us!

We entered a typical waiting room and were soon called back for the test. I could hardly breathe as the doctor turned on the ultrasound equipment. The test was short, as the doctor quickly confirmed that Hudson did indeed have a form of spina bifida called anencephaly. She explained to us that because the neural tube defect was at the top vertebrae of the spine, the brain and skull were failing to form correctly, and the baby would not be able to live outside of the womb.

The doctor recommended immediate termination of the pregnancy, since there was a zero percent chance of survival for him after birth. She said that we could just end this pregnancy now and try again. Tears streamed down my face at this confirmation. After the doctor left the room we again turned to prayer. My friend said she saw a stormy day at the beach, but the sun breaking through. We together committed Hudson to God.

So many questions flooded my mind. Could Hudson think if his brain was not forming? Would he have hair? Back at my doctor's office, we were again strongly encouraged to end Hudson's life. My doctor asked if an abortion was really causing harm based on Hudson's condition. He said he didn't think so. They told me if I chose to carry him I would be considered a high-risk pregnancy.

But this was our baby, a precious life created by God, a life with a purpose, a life that deserved to be treasured, nurtured and taken care of. Scared and broken, together we leaned on God, trusting in His provision, and walked forward. We never gave up hope. Maybe God would heal Hudson. Whatever happened, we realized his life was a gift.

Despite this resolve, a range of emotions were my constant companions: joy at the life inside my womb, yet sadness that I may never watch my baby grow up, and fear, wondering what labor would feel like. Could I endure the pain if it would end in the death of my precious baby?

Night was my rest from all these thoughts, and then in the morning reality would face me again as another day dawned. One of my friends gave me a scripture that would continue to be dear to me even to this day. Psalm 46:1-5 says:

"God is our refuge and strength, an ever-present help in trouble. Therefore, we will not fear, though the earth give way and the mountains fall into the heart of the sea, though its waters roar and foam and the mountains quake with their surging. There is a river whose streams make glad the city of God, the holy place where the Most High dwells. God is within her, she will not fall; **God will help her at break of day**,*"*

This was my morning work, to turn my thoughts from all the fears and pain to realize that God was with me in this new day. It was God who would give me the grace to meet whatever the day would bring.

Fall time in New England is beautiful. Spectacular colors adorn every tree. The air has that crisp fall feel - ideal conditions for an afternoon walk. Here again it was a choice to engage. Would I venture out to enjoy the leaves? I dreaded the thought of seeing someone on the walk that would ask about my baby? When was my due date? This was such a conflicted time in my heart. When hope should have been the strongest, I felt the weakest. It was like walking a tightrope that I did not have the strength to navigate.

But as we prayed and walked on, I began to embrace Hudson's life in the here and now. We had today! He could hear the sounds that were going on around me. He could hear the sound of my voice. He could experience the food that I ate, and the air that I breathed. I wanted to make these days full of good memories.

We took him to my favorite place, the ocean, so he could hear the wind, the waves and the cry of the seagulls. My friend and I took him to a nearby state park, where we could breathe the crisp fall air and hear the crunch of the fallen leaves.

We loved to feel Hudson kick and move. I would lay in bed just a little longer to enjoy his kicks. He loved to kick and move when Peter and Lupe came over to pray. He also loved to move during the singing at our church.

We treasured every move. I often interrupted Dwight's computer work so he could feel Hudson move as well.

Several of my treasured seminary professors confirmed this line of thinking. Dr. Aida Spencer wrote after spending time in prayer, "God gave me to understand that Hudson is loved by God and feels God's love in the womb...that he is living and enjoying life now."

Dr. Catherine Kroeger always checked in to see how I was doing. She gave me a music box to play for Hudson now. She said he would enjoy hearing the melody!

Before we found out about Hudson's condition, I had set aside several hours a day to make preparation for becoming a parent. We ordered materials that would give us the best insights into parenting. We listened to these tapes while driving in the car or doing things around the house. With the knowledge of Hudson's condition, we changed directions.

We now filled our time with prayer and things that we could do for Hudson now. I purchased a flowerpot to paint for him. As I painted the clay pot I prayed for him. I talked to him, read to him and sang to him.

Peter and Lupe came every day to pray with us and for us! Those were very special times of prayer. We asked God for the awareness of His presence in our day to day activities. We also asked for help, mercy and grace for all our needs. We lifted Hudson up to God, always asking for healing, and that God's name would be glorified.

One particular prayer time stands out in my memory. I was fighting a bad cold and had not slept well the night before. The verse that kept coming to mind throughout the night was Psalm 147:11, "The Lord takes pleasure in those who fear Him, in those who hope in His mercy." I knew that I could not continue without God's help, so I pleaded over and over again for God's mercy, knowing that my dependence on God pleased Him.

On that morning when Peter and Lupe came to pray, they brought eleven-year-old Jacob and nine-year-old Sunnie. While we prayed, the children colored get well pictures for me. They had no idea how much they would mean to me!

I believe that God directed their hands as they drew and colored purple and yellow flowers for me! These flowers expressed the heart of God to me. God had not forgotten me! He knew and understood my heartache and longings. He was there with me, and these pictures were to me a reminder of His promise to never leave me.

God's never-ending love would uphold me throughout the coming months. His grace would be sufficient for whatever lay ahead. His power was incomparable, and His mercies would be new every day. We continued to seek God and spend time in prayer.

During this time, I also continued my regular doctor appointments. Although they had not been supportive of me at the beginning, they were a great help as my pregnancy progressed. One appointment stands out. I needed to take a sugar test to check for gestational diabetes. After drinking the orange liquid, I had to wait for one hour. I felt confined in the waiting room as I waited for the time to pass, since I was not allowed to leave the room. I felt nervous, wondering what if anything this drink would do to my body. Dwight waited with me and distracted me by sharing the computer magazine he was reading.

After the test we went out to lunch at a Mexican restaurant. We placed our order, then I left the table, hoping for a quick stop in the restroom before our food arrived. Instead, I ended up getting locked in the bathroom stall because of a faulty door. At first, I panicked. Then I prayed for God's help. Our waitress knew about the faulty door, and when I was not coming back she came to check on me and let me out!

God used this experience to speak truth into my heart. What I really needed in my life was a deep awareness of God's presence, no matter where I was, or what was happening around me. Even if I was in a hard place, if I knew and felt God's presence, I could have peace. This is what we began to pray as we met and talked with family and friends.

My sister called every day to talk and pray. Letters and cards from dear friends came in the mail. My friends Leslie and Paul came every week to pray with us. This was before the days of email and texting, so it meant so much to me that even my friends who lived at a distance kept close in touch.

A prayer group of our seminary neighbors formed, and we prayed for Hudson and each other. It was during one of these prayer times about a month before Hudson would be born, that God showed Dwight a vision of Hudson's birth. Dwight said, "I saw Hudson being born whole, but the place he was in was full of brilliant light. I knew that the light was the presence of God, so I said that I believed that Hudson's birth would be glorious."

God sustained us through these times of prayer, giving us a new hunger and anticipation for times spent in His presence, alone and with other believers.

Time continued to march on. I had settled into a routine of study and prayer.

CHAPTER 3 HUDSON'S BIRTH

On Saturday, November 30th, after a busy day of Christmas shopping followed by prayer with Peter and Lupe, my water broke unexpectantly around 11:45pm. Even if Hudson didn't have a problem, this was too early for his arrival. My due date was not for ten more weeks! Now I was really unsure of what our path would be.

We called the doctor, and he told us we needed to head to the hospital. This was our local hospital close to our seminary apartment. We were greeted with kindness and given a room. The doctor that had been following my pregnancy was out of town. I was disappointed, but received the doctor on call from my office.

Upon his arrival he did an ultrasound. We saw Hudson's legs moving, but weren't able to view his head, as he was in the correct position for delivery.

Our doctor gave us several choices. We could stay here and let the labor continue, or we could transfer to the New England Medical Center by ambulance.

So many questions flooded our minds. Did Hudson still have the defect? What should be our next step? Should I have a C-Section? Should we go to Boston? Even if Hudson was healed, his birth would be ten weeks premature and he would need special care. New England Medical Center specialized in handling premature babies, so it would be the perfect place for him to be born.

After we talked and prayed we decided to go to Boston. We wanted to give Hudson the best care possible. We continued to press in to God in prayer for his healing. As long as Hudson's heart was beating we continued to hope and pray.

Even though it was late, two of our pastor friends met us at the hospital. They talked and prayed with us. One of my friends saw a picture as he prayed of Jesus holding a lamb in His arms. I held this comforting picture in my mind as we waited for them to transfer me to the ambulance.

The doctor also told us that by leaving the local hospital, we wouldn't have as much input into what we wanted for our care. We didn't fully understand what that meant, but we still felt this was the right decision for us.

At the local hospital a lot of information was presented to us based on their expectation of the outcome. For example, they told use they had trouble finding his heartbeat. Once I was in the ambulance, the nurse that accompanied me checked Hudson's heartbeat and assured me it was normal and strong.

As we entered this part of the journey, day and night merged together. We had no idea that this would last for three and a half long days!

Upon arrival at New England Medical Center, they hooked me up to numerous machines, monitoring my contractions and Hudson's heartbeat.

I did at one point have the opportunity to walk down the hallway, to see if that would accelerate my labor. When that didn't work they decided to give me Pitocin to speed up the labor process.

While all this was happening, my mom, my sister, and Dwight's parents left from Indiana and Michigan, and made the long journey by car to Boston, to be with us during our time of need. They left at a moment's notice. Their love and sacrifice to be with us during this time is still imprinted on our hearts today!

This part of the hospital stay was mainly filled with nurses caring for us and friends visiting. I remember one nurse in particular. She was my nurse when we first arrived. She was shocked that we were still there when she returned for her next shift.

My contractions were not normal. Instead of on and off contractions, I just felt one long contraction that never seemed to end. I finally decided to have an epidural to mask the labor pains.

The person who did my epidural did not put us at ease. I felt a lot of spiritual attack during this time. They gave me medication to help me sleep, but the drugs made me feel out of control of my emotions.

That night a friend of ours and Dwight knelt and prayed all night at my bedside. They prayed that God would fulfill the vision He had given Dwight during our prayer times. During this time, I did feel held in God's hand as I endured the long hours.

This part of the journey seemed to last forever, but in the midst of all this there were tender moments. We used this time to speak to Hudson about how much we loved him. We played him the music box my professor had given to him. Peter and Lupe came and brought a stuffed animal for Hudson and an outfit for him to wear. At the same time, they helped us speak tender words to him. Then a moment happened that would take time to unpack.

CHAPTER 4 HUDSON'S DEATH

It had now been three and a half days, and I was exhausted. Suddenly I started to feel nauseous. I remember saying the words, "Help me Jesus." Suddenly I was in brilliant light; a : different than I have seen on earth. The light held a purity that I could feel.

It was in this light that I sensed Hudson was there with me. I did not see him, but I knew. He was there and whole!

Then I remember being back in the hospital bed, and the doctors told me it was time to push.

For the next eight hours I was not fully present. I was aware of people coming and going in the room. Almost everyone I saw was surrounded in light. I also remember a table.

Here is what happened from Dwight's perspective. He was there with the nurse when I uttered the words, "Help me Jesus." That is when he saw me stop breathing. The nurse started calling my name, "Karen, Karen, Karen come back!" Since I was hooked up to so many machines, he also watched as my blood pressure plummeted. At this point, they made him leave the room and a team rushed in to resuscitate me.

He had no idea what was happening to me. He did however have strength to call friends to pray!

We found out later that even before the phone call, God had already awakened people to pray. God gave our friend Marjean Psalm 35 to pray:

"Contend, LORD, with those who contend with me; fight against those who fight against me. Take up shield and armor; arise and come to my aid. Brandish spear and javelin against those who pursue me. Say to me, "I am your salvation."
May those who seek my life be disgraced and put to shame; may those who plot my ruin be turned back in dismay. May they be like chaff before the wind, with the angel of the LORD driving them away; may their path be dark and slippery, with the angel of the LORD pursuing them. Psalm 35:1-6

She knew at that point she was not praying for Hudson's life, but for mine to be saved!

Marjean had asked an artist friend to paint a picture for me. This friend, having no idea I was in the hospital in labor, was awakened at this exact hour with a vision of what she was to paint. God gave her a picture of Hudson. In the picture Hudson is sitting on the shore. She said the buoy beside him had no rope because Hudson was heaven's baby.

That night my friend in Georgia had been praying for me, and received a vision. She saw angels at my bedside who took Hudson in their arms and took him to God. Later she told me the words that came to her were, "battle weary and bruised but not defeated." She had no idea that what she was seeing and hearing was happening as she prayed!

They used a machine to breathe for me for eight minutes, and then I began to breathe on my own again. I do not remember any of this. Dwight said that when they revived me they began asking me questions to assess my condition. I did not know where I was or why I was there. I asked if I had been in a car accident. I did not know what year it was, and did not recognize any of the nurses or doctors that had been with me constantly since my arrival. However, when they pointed to Dwight and asked who he was, I said, "That is Dwight, he is the most wonderful man in the world!" At that answer everyone was relieved.

I do not remember answering any of these questions.

In Dwight's words, "I was worried when they said they now wanted Karen to deliver Hudson, but it went very quickly. Hudson was a beautiful baby boy, even though I saw that he had the defect. They told me he had died in the process of birth. They clothed him and wrapped him in a blanket and gave him to me."
Dwight continued to be concerned about my condition. He watched as they carried out towels soaked in my blood. They also told him that I had lost some memory. For the next nine hours I asked Dwight the same questions over and over again, "How much did Hudson weigh?" "Did you call Ginger Lou?" "Were you there when Hudson was born?" I have no memory of speaking any words to Dwight.

Although Dwight was grateful to be able to hold Hudson's body, this part was extremely difficult for him. He was confronted not only with the fact that he had lost his son, but also his ability to communicate with me. How could he go on with me in this state?

During this time we were able to show Hudson's body to our families and Peter and Lupe, but most of the day we spent alone with him."

After about nine hours I remember a feeling, like waking up from a dream. I saw Dwight holding Hudson and wondered why?

The first words that came out of my mouth that made sense to Dwight were, "We need to say goodbye to Hudson's body. He is not here."

Dwight told me he was thinking the same thing. We prayed together and gave his body to the nurse.

I looked at my arms and wondered why there were IV's in both arms? Why was I receiving blood?

They were soon able to transfer me to a normal room. When we got to this room there was a window looking out to a courtyard with a beautiful Christmas tree. I commented to Dwight, "This room is not nearly as nice as the one we were in." Dwight was stunned at my words, since the other room had no windows and basically was just full of machines! We spent a long time talking about what we had each experienced. I realized that God had made the other room beautiful to me because of His presence!

I am not normally a person who sees visions, but later that day I had a vision of Hudson when I was praying. For a split second I saw him fully grown. He had Dwight's black hair and was strong and handsome.

The doctor who had supported me throughout my pregnancy personally called me to hear my voice and check on me. He had been informed of what had happened to me. When he later saw me for a follow up visit, he repeated over and over that it was a miracle that I was alive!

My family and friends continued to be a support. Dwight never left my side. The nurse that attended me when I stopped breathing came to see me on her own time. She said, "I just had to see with my own eyes that you were ok."

There was a lot of mystery surrounding what had happened to me. I had bruises all over my back and arms, and a cut on my throat.

I remember a doctor bringing another doctor in to look at the cut.

What they finally concluded based on my symptoms was that I had suffered an amniotic embolism.

This is a rare pregnancy complication where the amniotic fluid enters the blood stream and triggers a serious reaction, causing the blood to clot in the organs of the body, often causing lung and heart collapse, and massive bleeding. The condition is normally diagnosed by autopsy.

As I was literally bleeding to death they acted quickly. All the platelets in my blood were gone and had to be replaced. The blessing in my case is that the blood did not clot in my organs, causing certain death, but in my skin. This explained all the bruising on my arms and back, and the cut on my throat.

Since they had to replace all my platelets, it was the equivalent of receiving blood from over two hundred people. Because of the large amount given, they told me that I most likely had AIDS and hepatitis. I could not be tested for these diseases for at least several months. I would have to live with this reality until I got the results from the tests.

Even though I was surrounded by family, there are no words to describe how I felt being wheeled out of the hospital with no baby in my arms and my body so broken.

All the parting words of the doctors flooded my mind as we drove back to our apartment.

We arrived home to a clean apartment with a beautiful live Christmas tree full of white lights that our precious friends had gotten and decorated for us. It was such a gift of grace to my heart as tears streamed down my cheeks. In one of my darkest hours God was present, holding me and pouring out His grace; giving me strength for each moment.

I was not able to walk on my own. I still carried the bruises on my back and arms, and the unexplained cut on my throat. Not only was I stripped of my baby, but also what I thought was the ability to birth any more children.

I spent the first days in bed. My breast milk came in, which the doctor assured me was a good sign that my body was healing. However, this continued to act as a reminder of the pain and loss. I was reminded that Hudson was not there to receive the provision of food.

I did have enough strength to attend the burial on December 7th, but I had to be seated, since I was still too weak to stand.

On that cold December morning, God laid a beautiful covering of snow over everything, reminding me of His presence, purity, and holiness, which I had experienced just a few days before.

The funeral director had also taken time to cut fresh evergreen boughs to surround Hudson's casket. This was a reminder to us that life is eternal, and pointed us to the truth that Hudson was alive in heaven.

After the service, we went to my favorite beach to be quiet in God's presence and lean on His mercy.

The gravestone we chose had Jesus holding a lamb in His arms, just like the picture that God gave our friend at the beginning of my labor. We also inscribed the reference to the following verses on the stone:

"Therefore, if anyone is in Christ, the new creation has come: The old has gone, the new is here! All this is from God, who reconciled us to himself through Christ and gave us the ministry of reconciliation: that God was reconciling the world to himself in Christ, not counting people's sins against them. And he has committed to us the message of reconciliation. We are therefore Christ's ambassadors, as though God were making his appeal through us. We implore you on Christ's behalf: Be reconciled to God. God made him who had no sin to be sin for us, **so that in him we might become the righteousness of God.** *As God's co-workers we urge you not to receive God's grace in vain. For he says,*
"In the time of my favor I heard you,
and in the day of salvation I helped you."
I tell you, now is the time of God's favor, now is the day of salvation."
2 Corinthians 5:17-6:2

God continued to pour many blessings into our lives through meals, cards, and physically caring for me until I could walk on my own. With each act of service and thoughtfulness God was depositing grace in my heart.

A LULLABY FOR HUDSON

Snowdrops and roses, Hydrangea in bloom, scenting the sunrise and
stately at noon, and every leaf sustained in youth by the Master
Gardener's hand, traveling before us, he's entered that land.

Oh, city resplendent, queen of the sea, chocolates and diamond lovely
and free, and there he will sing and laugh and play till his joy outshines
the sun, live in love always and soon we will come.

Dear little baby, sweet little one, alive in the Spirit, the Father and
Son, for now he's returned his precious life to the land where he came
from at rest in the promise of thy Kingdom come.

--By Dr. Bill Spencer, December 14, 1996.

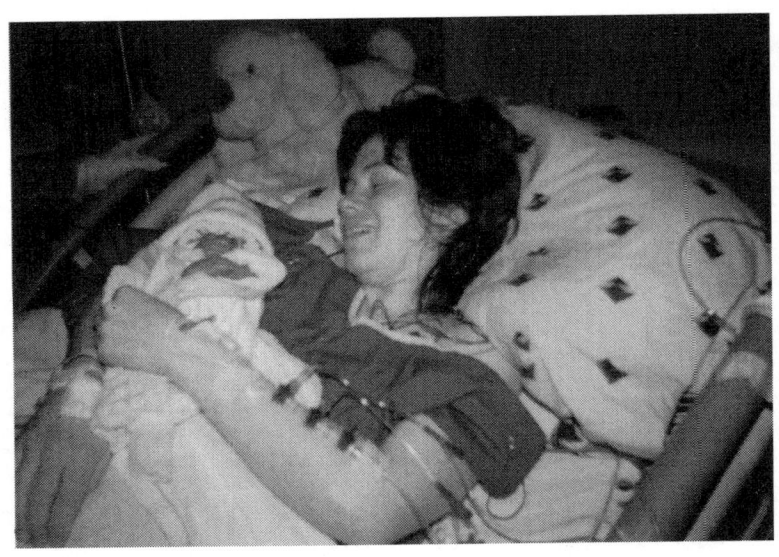

CHAPTER 5 THE RECOVERY

As I took to recounting the life of Hudson, I am still surprised at the emotions that well up in my heart even twenty-two years later! Loss is truly something that I we are not meant to recover from, but be enlarged by. As Jerry Sittser writes, "I believe that recovery from loss is an unrealistic and even harmful expectation, if by recovery we mean resuming the way we lived and felt prior to the loss."[1]

He gives the best analogy that I have heard, as he compares loss to a tree stump in his backyard. The stump is the reminder of the loss of what should have been growing and part of life. You cannot change the loss, but you can choose what you want to plant around it. Often the losses in our lives are like stumps, not visible at first notice, or covered by other things, but they still continue to be present and make the landscape of our lives different.[2]

The reality of the stump does not change. You cannot change or control the loss, but what you can control is how you react to the loss. Do you sit on the stump, or do you ask yourself, "How am I going to nurture the soil around the roots?" "What am I going to choose to plant around the stump?" If you don't have the strength to plant, ask others to come and help you dig and plant. Ask God to supply seeds for you to sow.

What would I plant around my stump?

I had a lot of time to think about this question as my body slowly regained strength.

As the days and weeks progressed, God was healing my body. I was also learning what I could do to support my body in the healing process.

I was eventually able to go on walks again. I loved looking at the trees in winter with their limbs pointed to the sky. I loved seeing all the intricacies of each branch. My heart could somehow identify with the branches, stripped of any signs of life, but still pointing to God in the midst of the cold.

Not only had I lost Hudson, but I also felt I had lost the ability to birth another baby. This was such a hard time to walk through. I felt that I would die if I had more children, but also, I longed so much to have a baby that I felt I would die of grief if I did not have another baby. No one could tell me what my chances were of having a healthy baby and a healthy delivery, because women who suffered my condition usually died.

During this time I wrestled with all these feelings, during prayer, on walks, at the ocean, and when studying. Looking back I now treasure this time I had to explore my feelings and be honest with God and my friends. I so appreciate all the friends who walked with me during this time and let me be where I was at emotionally. I also thought a lot about what I had experienced of the light of God. In the deep places of my heart I had always struggled, wondering if God loved me and I was truly His child. The light that I experienced surrounding me and covering me made me safe as I felt God's acceptance of me and of Hudson.

Romans 1:16-17 says, *"For I am not ashamed of the gospel, because it is the power of God that brings salvation to everyone who believes: first to the Jew, then to the Gentile. For in the gospel **the righteousness of***

God is revealed—a righteousness that is by faith from first to last, just as it is written: "The righteous will live by faith.""

Second Corinthians 5:21 says, "*God made him who had no sin to be sin for us, so that **in him we might become the righteousness of God**.*"

When we become a child of God, He gives us Christ's righteousness! It is not about what we do for God. We can do nothing to make ourselves acceptable before God. It is all about what God gives to us! Christ died on the cross and paid for our sins. We deserved death, but Christ took what we deserved, and by His death and resurrection we are now given **His righteousness** when we believe.

"*And this is the testimony: God has given us eternal life, and this life is in his Son. Whoever has the Son has life; whoever does not have the Son of God does not have life. I write these things to you who believe in the name of the Son of God so that you may know that you have eternal life.*" 1 John 5:11-13

Actually, experiencing this righteousness was a shining mercy in an otherwise dark time in my life.

Finally, the day came when I could take the AIDS test and the hepatitis test. Thankfully, both tests were negative. I was so relieved, and so thankful that God had protected me! Also, the testing showed that my body was healing well.

During Hudson's life God was growing in me a greater love for children and intimacy with Him. My experience in the delivery gave me a thankful heart to be alive, and also helped me to make decisions in light of the holiness of God. It also helped me choose to live in the light, even when surrounded by darkness.

Later, I would come to understand that the in-between time, the two years I waited before God placed another baby in our arms was also a gift. In this time, God was equipping us with keys for parenting the beautiful children He would eventually bring into our lives.

What did I do during this time to live, and not let the darkness of suffering and loss overtake me?

I was real. I am so thankful for Dwight and the patient friends who knew I was figuring out with God an uncharted way. They were there to let me walk at my own pace. I received the grace that I could understand, which was like refreshing streams on the parched ground of my heart. Twenty-two years later, I still have the list of those who brought food to us, the stacks of cards we received, and the handwritten notes from professors and the dean of Gordon Conwell Theological Seminary.

I ran to God in the darkness. God was speaking to me, but not on the topics that I was wanting to know about. Did I have AIDS? Would I ever have children? There was a thought that continued to ring in my heart as God remained silent about the questions that haunted my heart. Finding hope was not in looking back. It was not seeing the setting sun and trying to live in its light. Finding hope was choosing to enter the darkness of the night so you could find the sunrise.[3] The past, even if painful, is familiar. But, choosing to face the darkness of your present and move forward is the path that will eventually lead to hope fulfilled.

I retreated. I looked for places that would help me connect with God. I spent time outdoors and at the ocean. The ocean was the place I most often visited. The rhythmic sound of the waves washed over my heart, reminding me that God keeps His promises!

I loved to feel the sand on my feet and the wind in my hair. Looking out on the vastness of the ocean brought comfort to my heart, as I was reminded of God's greatness and unending love. I took joy in the fact that you cannot see an end to the horizon. I also loved the surprises of finding an interesting shell or rock.

I was always listening and seeking my beautiful heavenly Father, who was my constant source of hope. He showed up in the details of my life, and assured me that He cared about the big things, even if He didn't speak to me about them.

Knowing that God cared about the little things in my life would later become a source of comfort to me. I came to understand that parenting in many ways is all about the details of life.

I saw that the skills God was teaching me would help me to be an effective parent. As a parent I would need to continue to be real about the struggles I would face. I would need to face pain, and also find ways to be refreshed on the journey. However, the most important thing I learned was to always keep my relationship God as my highest priority.

CHAPTER 6 SARA NOELLE & HANNAH ELIZABETH

A year later we were able to ask God for another child. To our delight, we found out I was pregnant when we were on a ministry trip in Toronto, Canada!

While I carried my second baby, I again daily treasured the life inside of me. But again I faced many struggles as we approached the normal tests and appointments.

During this time, God was teaching me, and giving me truths to live and parent by:

God was teaching me to face my fears. In order for me to embrace the life of my baby, I would have to face a path uncharted. This was a daily walk, and one where I needed others to pray with me and for me. We are not meant to live life alone. God made us to be in relationship with Him and each other.

But what do you do with your fears? First, acknowledge what has you paralyzed, second, pray about your fears, and third, find others who will pray for you as well. Finally, ask God for your next step and take it!

Parenting is a big task, and we need God to give us wisdom for each stage of our children's lives. Each stage will bring new challenges and new fears, but the important thing is to face what is before you, and ask God for the way through.

God was teaching me to hear His voice and listen for His wisdom. God's wisdom will bring life and hope to your situation. Ask for divine strategies that will produce good fruit in your life. We live in a world full of information, but having wisdom is knowing what piece of knowledge fits the pieces of your life together. If we lack wisdom, all we need to do is ask God. He will give us all that we need! James 1:5 says, "If any of you lacks wisdom, you should ask God, who gives generously to all without finding fault, and it will be given to you." So ask, and then look for how God will answer!

God was teaching me to pay attention to my thoughts and my words. I was learning to monitor my thoughts. What picture did I have in my mind? Was I thinking about all the things that could go wrong, or was I meditating on God's promises, and the good things that He has in store for me? Also, I was learning to make sure that the words that I spoke matched the good picture that I was holding in my mind. I worked on always speaking words of life and hope. I love this quote by Pastor Bill Johnson, "I can't afford to have a thought in my head about me that God does not have in His."[1]

God continued to be present as we walked through each day of our second baby's life in the womb. Before we had the ultrasound, God gave Dwight a vision of a beautiful little girl in a red dress in front of him, opening her arms for a hug. As he took her into his embrace, he said, "I love you Sara." We were not surprised when the results of the ultrasound showed that I was carrying a baby girl!

When the time came for me to deliver her, I again faced many emotions. Despite all the preparation and prayer, I felt so weak facing Sara's delivery. My midwife knew about everything that happened with Hudson. She helped me to have courage to push when the time came. There was a part of my heart that was still holding on to fear. She spoke the words, "Karen, you can do this! Sara is healthy and you can deliver her safely." Holding on to these words, I delivered Sara Noelle at 2:14 PM on December 12th. Then just eighteen months later, Hannah Elizabeth was born on July 15th! Hannah, God's beautiful gift of grace, weighed in at 6 pounds 11ounces. She was a joy from the beginning, and a constant companion for Sara. They did everything together! Whether it was a class or a new activity, everything was easier having your sister by your side! My heart overflowed with thankfulness for the beautiful garden that God was growing and allowing me to nurture!

CHAPTER 7 JESSIE

Hudson was not my only heavenly baby.

After Sara and Hannah, I longed for more children. I with the darkness from birthing Hudson, but I felt like my heart had found its calling in being a mother.

This is where the story of Jessie's life comes into our family.

In March 2002, our days were filled with prayer and long talks. Dwight's words rang in my heart, "Children are always a blessing from God." Because of all that we had been through, the decision to have another baby was a big one for both of us. The verse of Scripture that kept coming to my mind was, *"And without faith it is impossible to please God, because anyone who comes to Him must believe that He exists and that He rewards those who earnestly seek Him."* Hebrews 11:6

Opening our hands and hearts meant a big step of faith for both of us. We moved forward, trusting in God's presence, provision and care.

There were doctor appointments for me, making sure that my body was ready to carry another child. There were diet changes. I was willing to give up foods that would adversely affect my blood sugar levels, and I began counting carbohydrates. I wanted to give a child the best place to grow. Our hearts were open, waiting on God.

On June 9, 2002, before a full morning of yard sales, I took a pregnancy test and found out that a new baby had entered our lives!

All of my early doctor appointments progressed normally, but when it was time to hear the baby's heartbeat my midwife could not find it. She assured me that sometimes the heartbeat is just hard to locate, and knowing what I had been through previously she scheduled an ultrasound for me the next day. The technician who performed the test was very kind to us. She took her time with the test, but as she showed us the baby's small body we all saw there was no beating heart.

Things progressed quickly and they scheduled me for surgery. My sister flew out to help us with Sara and Hannah. This time my body did have to recover, but it was not attacked as it had been delivering Hudson. It was my soul that needed care. This loss hit a tender spot in my heart, as I realized my part in Jessie's life was now over. See Appendix A to read more about Jessie's life story.

Sara and Hannah were such a comfort to me during this time. I enjoyed caring for them and holding them in my arms.

Then more losses followed. Dwight lost his job, and after prayer we decided we should move back to the Midwest, to be closer to our extended family. God gave Dwight a vivid dream. In the dream he saw a FedEx truck, and a man handing him his next job offer. We took this as confirmation that God was moving us. We put our house on the market, and it sold with three full-price offers two days before Christmas, even after a heavy rainstorm caused flooding in our basement! Even our realtor was surprised at this response. So, we would leave New England without a job or a place to live. Thankfully, Dwight's parents in Michigan gave us a place to stay until God revealed the next step. My parents came to help us with the move, and provided us a place to store our belongings until the next step would unfold.

This was not an easy move for me. I loved New England, the ocean, and the beautiful house that God had given to us. I remembered when we were looking for a house, and we stopped at this particular one. Dwight waited in the car with Sara and Hannah, and I was only in the house for a few minutes. I came back to the car and said, "I love this one!" Dwight agreed, and when we did the home inspection I was surprised to find details about the house that I had not even initially seen. It had everything on my wish list and more! One of my favorite parts of the house was the back room, which was full of windows looking out on a beautiful yard. From the time we moved in, I continued to personalize the house.

One way I did this was to take up the craft of stenciling. So much of what you do as a mother is repeated activity. You wash the dishes and clean the kitchen, only to have to do it all over again the next day. I longed to be able to do an activity that would stay. This is what prompted me to learn to stencil with paint and detailed masks, which made beautiful designs. This was very satisfying to me, as my work remained to be enjoyed every time I walked into the room! I did an ocean theme in the bathroom, and lighthouses on either side of the fireplace. We also made a custom window seat to match our couch. We loved making our house a home.

This was also a hard move for me in other ways. I was unsure if and when we could have another child, which felt like an added weight to my already saddened heart.

Suffering and loss will come to each of our lives during our journey here on earth, but God will never forsake His children. He uses the battle and the attacks to help us know new levels of His grace and glory. No matter what storm you are in, no matter what darkness you face, Jesus can and will deliver you if you run to Him.

CHAPTER 8 AN EXAMPLE TO FOLLOW

Second Corinthians 1:10-11 says, "*God has delivered us from such a deadly peril, and he will deliver us again. On him we have set our hope that he will continue to deliver us, as you help us by your prayers. Then many will give thanks on our behalf for the gracious favor granted us in answer to the prayers of many.*"

As we have walked down the path of parenting, we have learned again the importance of prayer. Even in days of great trial and testing, God is upholding, moving and working. We are not alone. My prayer continued to be for more of God.

Before I move on with my story, let's take a closer look at these verses in their larger context. In Second Corinthians chapter one, we are given a window into how Paul handled loss and suffering as he followed Christ. His words and example give us keys to dealing with the suffering that comes our way as we journey with God through this life.

Throughout the book of Second Corinthians, Paul talked a lot about his past sufferings. He did this to show that his relationship with God was real, and his ministry was authentic. Throughout the book of Second Corinthians, Paul recalled many of the things he suffered. For example, Second Corinthians 4:8-9 says, "We are hard pressed on every side, but not crushed; perplexed, but not in despair; persecuted, but not abandoned; struck down, but not destroyed."

In Second Corinthians 6:4-10, Paul spoke again of afflictions, hardships, calamities, and beatings. He also wrote about times of imprisonments, riots, labors, and sleepless nights. In Second Corinthians 11:24-25, he recorded that five times he received from the Jews forty lashes minus one, three times he was beaten with a rod, and once he was stoned.

In Second Corinthians chapter one, Paul described a specific time of intense suffering in his ministry. The exact events of this time of suffering are hard to pin down. The point that is most important in these verses is that Paul did not forget this great time of suffering in his life, and he did not want his readers to forget either.

Second Corinthians 1:8-11 reads, "*We do not want you to be uninformed, brothers and sisters, about the troubles we experienced in the province of Asia. We were under great pressure, far beyond our ability to endure, so that we despaired of life itself. Indeed, we felt we had received the sentence of death. But this happened that we might not rely on ourselves but on God, who raises the dead. He has delivered us from such a deadly peril, and he will deliver us again. On him we have set our hope that he will continue to deliver us, as you help us by your prayers. Then many will give thanks on our behalf for the gracious favor granted us in answer to the prayers of many.*"

How did Paul talk about this intense time of suffering in the present? He was honest about what he had experienced and how hard it had been.

Paul explained how he felt as he went through this intense time of suffering. Look with me at the second half of verse eight. First, he said that they were under great pressure. To really understand the impact of these words, picture in your mind a ship that is overloaded and at risk of sinking. This great pressure on them was far beyond their ability to endure, so that they despaired even of life. The Greek word used for "despaired" is a word that is rarely used in the New Testament. It communicates the idea that there was no exit. Imagine a maze with no way out. On every side is a dead end, and there is no path to follow. They had no resources left. Paul went on to say in verse nine that they felt the sentence of death in their hearts.[1]

Death was staring them in the face. Only the one who has power over death could deliver them. But this is the kind of God they served - a God who can raise the dead!

God was their only hope! He alone had the power to deliver them. The only way out of this impossible situation was God's intervention.

Paul reemphasized this in these verses, when he talked of his total dependence on God, and not on himself. He recounted God's deliverance from the deadly peril in verse 10, "But this happened that we might not rely on ourselves but on God, who raises the dead. He has delivered us from such a deadly peril."

In the midst of his suffering, Paul found hope in God. So we have seen that Paul did not forget about his past suffering, and he honestly talked of the difficulty of those sufferings in the present. But what about future suffering? How did Paul look at the future in light of his past and present? What did he know and understand about God that gave him hope to keep pressing on?

Paul looked to the future with hope. God is a deliverer and a rescuer. He knew that God does not change. He is the same yesterday, today, tomorrow and forever (Hebrews 13:5)! As God had delivered him in the past, he could expect God's continued deliverance in the future!

In verse ten, Paul repeated the verb *"deliver"* three times for emphasis, *"He has **delivered** us from such a deadly peril, and he will **deliver** us. On Him we have set our hope that he will **continue to deliver** us."* God was the one who rescued him from his impossible situation, so Paul's hope was fully on God for the future. God would prove faithful, and this is what he was banking his hope on. Paul did not expect that he would never encounter suffering of this magnitude again, but he did expect God to deliver him, just as he had done before.

"On Him we have set our hope that he will continue to deliver us, as you help us by your prayers. Then many will give thanks on our behalf for the gracious favor granted us in answer to the prayers of many."
2 Corinthians 1:10b-11

It is important to note Paul's dependence on prayer as he hoped in God. He knew that God would deliver, but God's deliverance would come as the result of prayer. The grammar of this sentence points us to this fact. "As you help us with your prayers" is a phrase explaining how the deliverance of God would come. The deliverance would come through prayer, and the result of the answered prayers would be thanksgiving. As John Piper wrote in his book Future Grace, *"Gratitude exults in the past benefits of God and says to faith, 'Embrace more of these benefits for the future, so that my happy work of looking back on God's deliverance may continue.'"*[2]

Let us review where we have been. First, we looked at Paul's past sufferings, and saw that he did not forget about them. In the present he was strikingly honest about how hard his sufferings had been. Lastly, we looked at how Paul viewed the future, and we see that he hoped in God and asked for prayers that God would continue to be his deliverer.

There are several ways these verses can be a help to you. If you are not facing suffering or hardship, pray for those who are. If you have suffered, ask yourself what your past deliverances are, and write them down. Remember what God has done in your life. In the present, examine your view of God. Do you know God as your rescuer, your deliverer, and your help? For the future, place your hope in God, and enlist the prayers and partnership of others.

Paul lived and conducted his entire ministry by the grace of God. His dependence wasn't on himself, but on God who would deliver him by His grace. Follow Paul's example in the way he conducted his ministry. Live with hope, asking God for His gracious deliverance. As you do, keep the third stanza of the hymn Amazing Grace echoing in your mind: "Through many dangers, toils, and snares I have already come. Tis grace that brought me safe thus far, and grace will lead me home."

One thing is certain: as we journey through this life we will all experience suffering and loss. This is why Paul's attitude is so important to understand and follow.

I heard a testimony on a radio station that spoke of this very topic. As we began to listen to the voice of the man, immediately his story grabbed my attention. He was explaining how he had lost his family in a tragic airplane accident, and the grief that followed. One particular comment he made stood out to me. He said people would comment on his suffering and say, "Well, God must have really wanted to get your attention." He went on to say how deeply those words hurt him. At the time of the accident he was walking closely with God. He was not living in sin or running away from God.

No one is immune from suffering and loss. Jesus said in this world we will have trouble, but to take heart because He has overcome the world (John 16:33). Suffering touches all of our lives. We need to know that when we encounter trouble that we have a deliverer!

Keep building your relationship with God. He will never leave you nor forsake you!

During my times of suffering, God not only upheld me, but the grace I received was personal. This grace brought healing and strength to me, because God understood how the loss of Jessie and the move fit into my life story. This is why no loss is processed the same, because no one shares our history. The losses we encounter come into the context of our lives. For example, maybe this is your third time being rejected for a job position. When faced with another rejection you could feel paralyzed with grief. But, someone else may see the rejection as a gift, because they wanted the other job that was being offered to them.

Losses are like tree stumps. They are a reminder of what was in the past, and what could have been if death or destruction had not entered your life.

Therefore, like Paul be honest about your loss. Everyone will encounter situations differently, so that is why you need to understand why your loss is hard for you. For me, leaving Massachusetts and the ocean was very difficult. But maybe someone else in the same situation would have welcomed the move. Maybe they didn't like their current town and were looking for a new start. In that case, they would welcome a move to a new state.

Your loss happens in the context of your life, and you need to process the loss inside your story. There are many Psalms that put words of grief into strong language. Maybe you would not feel comfortable being this raw or honest before God. Try to find a Psalm that matches your heart's cry, and express those words of grief to God. Then wait for His response.

As I was honest, and processed the losses of this season of my life, God was teaching me and giving me truths to live and parent by:

God was teaching me that loss is real. He was helping me to be honest with how I was feeling, and encouraged me to speak to Him from the depths of my heart. Honesty in our family relationships brings opportunities for growth and connection. It also opens the door for hope.

This lesson would become important in helping my children deal with losses that they encountered. For example, how would you deal with not getting the part in the musical you wanted with all your heart, or being asked to dance as an understudy for an entire year? How would you react to a disappointing test score, or placing last in a tennis match? The same lessons apply. We have learned as a family to take these losses to God and hear His words to us. At first I was reluctant to ask God about these painful life moments, but I have been overwhelmed and comforted as we have seen God bring life into the broken places of our hearts.

God was teaching me that the present moment is precious, even if it is painful. I needed to learn to be present in the moment, not regretting the past or wishing it back, and not fearing the future. I needed to realize that it is God's breath in my lungs right now. This present moment is a gift from God, reminding me that God's name is I AM. I love the quote, "Yesterday is history, tomorrow is mystery, today is a gift." Each day is a gift to be treasured!

I have always loved to journal and scrapbook. Therefore I incorporated capturing thoughts and memories as part of our homeschool. Each year we worked on filling a binder, capturing all of our most important moments and work. Everything that went into the binder was put in a plastic sleeve, not only preserve it, but also to show that it was important and worth saving.

God was teaching me to look for His provision. Since we did not know what job Dwight would get or what city we would end up in, this made for a very uncertain time in our lives. God was teaching me to trust that He would carry us one day at a time. God's strength often came in unexpected ways, so I found it important to pay attention to what God provided every day. I needed God's wisdom for my present reality. I needed Him to give us ideas to nurture our children during the transition, and to give us the next steps for our family. God showed me that we needed to remember to laugh. We needed to keep a regular routine as much as possible, even while everything around us was changing. Mostly, God showed me that we needed to remind ourselves and our children that He had good plans for our family.

CHAPTER 9 JONATHAN EDWARD

God never let us down! However, it would be nine months before we would find ourselves putting the key inside the door to our new home in Wheaton, Illinois! It was another birthing as we searched and waited for God to open doors for us. I remember praying and crying after a church service during the transition. Someone came up to me and said that God had brought about many answers to prayer in my life, and God wanted me to remember those victories!

Our new home in Wheaton had beautiful built in bookshelves. The first time I saw them, I realized that they would not be a home for books, but for answers to prayer! Each shelf now contains an object that reminds me of a prayer God answered, or a work He has done in my life. The FedEx package that contained Dwight's new job offer was one of the first things we added to our new bookshelves. It was not only an answered prayer, but the fulfillment of Dwight's dream!

We remember well the day that Dwight's dream came to pass. We had been in Chicago for the job interview process, and now the official job offer was being delivered by FedEx! The delivery man was surprised, but happy to get his picture taken when we explained to him what was inside the package.

During the months of transition before the job offer arrived, we treasured the words that God spoke to us as we waited. Sometimes our hearts can hear better in different contexts. During the time of transition, God helped us understand the importance of where we should place our focus. When we left Massachusetts, we had to go to where God would show us. Therefore, our focus was not on a destination, but our focus was on the presence of God. This would be a lesson that would bring comfort to my heart several years later.

One particular word stands out that was given to us by the pastor of a church we were attending during this time. He said he felt that God was saying that things would take longer than we wanted, but that the move was about our children. The one thing that we always hear about Wheaton is that this city is a great place to raise a family! We have had so many amazing connections and opportunities for our family to learn and grow in this area of the country!

Our family expanded on October 16, 2004, as Jonathan Edward was born! He was a blessing from day one! God carried us through the days of my pregnancy, still with much prayer! The week before he was born, friends from a previous church came to the church we were currently attending. They said that God had spoken to them that I needed prayer for the birth of my baby, and they were being obedient to His voice!

God also gave me wonderful friends to walk alongside me here in Illinois. I did wait until the very last minute to go to the hospital, as I was dreading a hospital delivery without my midwife. But God was going before me and preparing the way. The nurse who assisted in the delivery was from Massachusetts, and was very kind to us!

Jonathan was a joy from the very beginning. We had fun watching him go through each stage of development. My heart was full! I felt so much closure and restoration with the birth of Jonathan. I enjoyed every minute of his newborn days. I treasured the times when I rocked him to sleep.

CHAPTER 10 ARRON

With a ten, nine and four-year-old, my days were busy and full of life. I enjoyed searching out and finding what worked best for each of my children. I wanted to help them learn and grow according to how God created them!

Sara always loved details, spending hours on homeschool projects. Make anything a game for Hannah, and she was instantly engaged and spreading fun to all around her. Jonathan was an inventor and idea man right from the very beginning!

Then suddenly, unexpectantly, I again found myself pregnant. I had lots of feelings to process when I saw that the pregnancy test was positive. I thought we had put the closing chapter on my childbearing years, but now a new life was again inside of me!

We sat down to breakfast one morning shortly after I found out about our new child. Sara told me about a dream she had the night before. She said, "Mom, I dreamed you were pregnant with another baby, and I was so happy because now I would have someone to play with." I took this opportunity to tell her that her dream was true and that indeed she was to have a new brother or sister in April. My actual due date was to be Good Friday of the coming year!

I scheduled an appointment for a blood test to confirm that everything was going as anticipated. They checked my hormone levels and said they were perfect!

We all joined in the excitement and let friends and family know, and of course asked for prayer! I had given away all my baby things, so I began planning for this new little one.

I was feeling all the normal pregnancy feelings. This was now my sixth time to receive the good news of a child in my womb!

A few weeks later we were at a favorite toy store to buy a present for an upcoming birthday party when I began to feel very thirsty. This was unusual for me. We purchased the item we wanted and headed home. I still continued to feel parched. I tried eating some of the foods that I was craving, and then laid down to rest.

I made an appointment with my doctor, as this new symptom puzzled me and I just wanted to get checked out. Our doctor was wonderful, and assured me that with so many hormone changes happening thirst was often a side effect, and there was nothing to be concerned about. He said that he would conduct an ultrasound and do a blood test, just to make sure everything was progressing normally.

As he hooked the machine up I again felt many emotions, but waited in silence as he reached the wand towards my abdomen. We saw the egg sack and the signs of life in my womb. We were not able to see the heartbeat, but my doctor assured us this was totally normal, as the pregnancy was just in the beginning weeks. I was relieved to see with my eyes that I was carrying another child, and not just feeling changes in my body. The doctor even gave me an ultrasound picture! This was a gift from God that I now treasure!

A few days later I received a call from the doctor. When I heard his voice, my heart sank. I almost could not take in the words he spoke. "Your hormone levels are dropping." "You will lose the baby." He asked me to call him in a few days, and we would decide the next step.

I reached out for prayer, and hoped that maybe this was all just a mistake, but I remembered the thirst and the other signs. Even my own body was saying that things were not as they should be.

God brought a precious friend into my life that had gone through a similar loss. She prayed with me and answered many of my questions. I did not look forward to delivering this baby. I never liked the term miscarriage because of all I had been through, and still to this day I do not like the word. Whether a baby is a few days old, or is born and grows to an old age, the baby is still a unique life, having purpose and a destiny to fulfill.

The doctor told me that I most likely would not have to have surgery, and my body would be able to handle losing the baby. This is what happened. God brought me through without going to the hospital, for which I was extremely grateful. Dear friends in Arizona, along with other precious friends and family prayed me safely through this time.

If Hudson's life brought with it an attack against my body, and Jessie's life brought with it an attack against my soul, Arron's life brought with it an attack against my spirit. Even though this child was in my life for a few short weeks, the storm in my heart would be the most devastating. So many questions filled my mind? How could God let me end this way? How could I begin with loss and end with loss?

The darkness was overwhelming. Tears did not even come, just groaning. This was a time of great heartache in my life. There were other losses going on in my ministry, which added to my sorrow. But God assured me that even if things I hoped for felt like they were being stripped away, I would eventually gain my true heart's desire, which is increased intimacy with Him.

I had to take everything at a very slow pace. It was very hard for me to be around babies. I would often find myself in tears. Once when I was holding Jonathan, he asked me why I was "raining" on him.

I positioned myself to receive from God. I attended many conferences and worship times. I felt that God was calling me to surrender to mystery.

Then there were times when God brought unexpected healing to my heart.

One time we were praying with a small group of people that did not know my story. One of the men in the prayer time looked up at us with a puzzled expression after we were done praying. He said that he saw a vision of a baby in heaven on a swing set, and he thought it was my baby! This was such a blessing to my heart.
God also gave me a gift through a friend. She also had a baby in heaven, and said that God showed her a vision of her child and one of our children playing together in heaven. I had never thought about the idea that our earthly friendships could also have an impact on our heavenly family!

One speaker at a healing conference I was attending brought great comfort to my heart. He spoke of his own unanswered questions. He talked of how he placed them in a cloud to be stored away, until he could ask God when he got to heaven. The thing that impacted me was when he talked about where he placed his cloud. His cloud remained off to the side, and he never let it come between him and God. This allowed him to have a childlike faith, even in the face of unanswered prayers and unfulfilled dreams. [1]

How we named our sixth baby is very special to me. I wanted to make a book for this baby, just like I did for Hudson and Jessie (The full book is in Appendix B). I was not sure what I would write in the book, since this baby was with us for such a short time. I decided to ask Sara and Hannah to ask God for a picture to draw for the book. Sara said that she saw what she thought was the hand of God holding a shining light in-between His fingers, and Hannah drew the baby in heaven.

We named this baby Arron, which is a form of Aaron, which means "shining light." God also impressed on my heart Philippians 2:15:

"...so that you may become blameless and pure, "children of God without fault in a warped and crooked generation. Then you will shine among them like stars in the sky."

This brought me full circle to the lesson that would be a thread running throughout all the losses in my life: **Where would I chose to place my focus?**

What picture would I keep in my mind? Would it be of the darkness that sought to overwhelm me? Or would I choose to focus on my "shining light," Arron, who brought me the gift of learning more about my heart. I learned to treasure every moment of life, making it the best it could be. I was also reminded that heaven is real.

God showed me that in order to walk forward in hope, my focus needed to be on His presence. This is the same lesson He taught me so many times during the birthing of all my children!
God's name is Emmanuel, God with us (Isaiah 7:14)! I am not alone. He is present in my life! I saw that this was not just a truth

that is to be remembered at Christmas, but one that I needed to cherish with reverence!

I was not ending my childbearing years in loss. Instead I was focused on God's presence, on living in the light of the holiness and purity of God. God was placing in my heart a stronger hunger for His purity and living in His light!

CHAPTER 11 WALKING IN THE DARKNESS - FOCUSED ON THE LIGHT

It was a precious revelation that God was calling me to keep my focus on His presence. However, I still needed God to minister to my broken heart. I again entered a season of healing as I walked forward.

During this time, God was teaching me and giving me truths to live and parent by.

I believe that the following keys He gave me during this time not only helped me walk forward and gain healing, but are also keys that parents need today to raise children who live in our current culture!

God was teaching me that I need assistance in healing my heart. Not only do we need to be honest about our losses, but sometimes loss is so great that your honest prayers are not enough. God has given many forms of healing prayer that can help you know His presence and help in these dark times.

Parenting can be challenging. We need the help of others who have gone before us to share the wisdom they have gained. Having mentors has been a key in my life to help me not only heal, but find solid ground to walk on.

For example, sometimes we face obstacles as parents that are impossible to figure out. I know the feeling of seeing what is not working, but not knowing which part of my life needs to change.

When Jonathan started homeschooling, I just assumed all the methods that worked with Sara and Hannah would be just as effective with Jonathan. However, when Jonathan and I both became frustrated with his school work, I began to search for answers. I sought God's wisdom. I attended a lot of trainings and read a lot of books along the way. Looking back, I am not sure which of the keys opened the door for Jonathan to grow in leaps and bounds in his school work. But I know it was some combination of all the things we tried. Plus, because of my searching I have now completed the Brain Gym training! I also became a certified Structure of Intelligence examiner! I learned so much about how our bodies impact our learning and thinking. It was worth the search to find answers! There is always hope. You just need to be able to ask the right questions and find the right pieces of the puzzle to bring your world together!

We live in a culture full of information, but sometimes that makes it even more confusing to find the solution to a problem. That is where having a mentor or coach can be a great help. A coach can help you find the key that fits, and opens the door to helping your family thrive. Make sure you find the help you need rather than suffering alone.

God was teaching me the importance of fasting. When you are not able to get a breakthrough in an area, fasting is a great tool. Fasting moves mountains! When we fast, it is not to manipulate or force God to do something. Fasting needs to be done with the attitude of "I don't have to, but I get to." I have never embarked on a fast where God has not given me a blessing in some way! (Make sure you check with your doctor before doing your first fast.)

I believe parents today need to ask God for tenacity. They need to not settle for the good, but find the best for their children.

God was teaching me to embrace mystery. The book of Job is the story of how Job faced overwhelming loss, and how he dealt with the loss. It is interesting to me that God answered Job's questions with questions, and that Job heard God's voice speaking these questions to him. Job stayed near to God in his sufferings.

Instead of disillusionment and living with unanswered prayer, I needed to embrace the reality there are some things we will never understand on this side of heaven. This is easier said than done, but by asking God for the grace to surrender my need to know, I found Him daily strengthening me. God used many creative ways to show me that He knew my pain, and remembered my past hurts and losses.

There have been more times than I can count in these last twenty-two years that God has given me what I call targeted grace. This is where God does something that is so personal it goes deep into your heart. The targeted grace touches a place in your heart that is bleeding and raw, and applies a balm to that specific area. One example of this in my life was the way God spoke to me through the Psalms. I started to pay attention to the times I woke up in the middle of the night. The time would represent a chapter in the Psalms. I would then read and ponder that Psalm during the next day. On the day that would have been Hudson's twenty first birthday, God woke me up at 3:50 AM, which pointed me to Psalm 35! This was the Psalm God used to awaken my friend to pray for my life to be spared when Hudson was born. It closes with, "My tongue will proclaim your righteousness, your praises all day long." Psalm 35:28

In 2017 our family vacation took us to Vermont for a week with good friends, and then on to Maine for more hiking and adventure. During our week at Acadia National Park, we enjoyed getting to know the couple who occupied the cabin next to ours. The husband was actually born on Mount Desert Island, so he told us many interesting things about the Island, and fun things to see and do. Before we left, his wife gave me two white roses from a bouquet she had purchased. I was blessed by this kind gift, because we planned to leave early in the morning, so we could stop by Hudson's grave on our way home. I looked forward to leaving the flowers at Hudson's grave, one for Jessie and one for Arron. This would be the first time to visit Hudson's grave since Arron had entered and left our lives.

When we arrived at the grave, God opened my eyes to see something I had never seen before. As I laid the roses on the grave, God highlighted the lambs on Hudson's gravestone. In the past, visiting Hudson's grave always brought up a lot of emotions for me, and my eyes always focused on Jesus holding the lamb. Today my eyes were drawn to two more lambs - a lamb beside Jesus, and another lamb on the right side of the stone! There were three lambs - one for Hudson, one for Jessie and one for Arron! God brought a supernatural comfort to my heart in that moment, as all my children were remembered by Him! I was amazed that God had kept this from my eyes until now when it would be a source of comfort and not of fear. God is my gentle shepherd who will never leave me nor forsake me!

God was teaching me to be aware of the spiritual battle. We are not on neutral ground. Our enemy's desire is that our lives would end in destruction. He wants to kill new growth in our lives, and keep us from moving forward with the dreams God has placed in our hearts.

When losses come, this is the perfect breeding ground for lies to be spoken into our lives. Circumstances or the loss itself will validate the lie, and make you more vulnerable to believing more lies. It becomes a slippery slope.

During times of loss it is imperative to put on the armor of God described in Ephesians 6:14-17:

"Stand firm then, with the belt of truth buckled around your waist, with the breastplate of righteousness in place, and with your feet fitted with the readiness that comes from the gospel of peace. In addition to all this, take up the shield of faith, with which you can extinguish all the flaming arrows of the evil one. Take the helmet of salvation and the sword of the Spirit, which is the word of God."

I believe that understanding God's armor will benefit both parents and children, highlighting to them how to live in victory and hope! This is why the last three chapters of this book will contain a detailed look into the armor of God.

CHAPTER 12 ALL MY CHILDREN

A very special gift I received from my dear friend is my broken heart necklace. It is a silver heart with a fern imprinted on it. There are three holes in the heart, each one representing one of my heavenly babies. The designer wrote about how and why she imprinted the fern on the heart. She said it was "created from an actual live fern and represents the beauty of life, the unfolding of miracles and the celebration of all living things." I love to wear this necklace, as it reminds me of all the children God has given us, and the gift that each one has given or is giving to our lives.

Hudson awakened me to prayer, and helped me understand the gift of the righteousness of Christ that makes me acceptable to God. Experiencing God's light has influenced the way that I live, and continues to lead me to make choices in light of the purity of God.

Jessie taught me to treasure the moment and to bring my broken heart to God. Jessie also taught me that life is strong, and life is fragile.

Arron gave me the gift of focus and surrender. Arron also helped me see that every moment you have with your children is precious, so you need to make it the best it can be. Children are a gift from God and need to be stewarded with honor and care. They are often your teachers as well, to help you know new facets of God's love.

Each of my heavenly babies have given me a gift, and left a legacy that has changed me. They have helped me to treasure my earthly children more, to pray more, and to help my earthly children grow into all that God has called them to be.

At the writing of this book, Sara has just turned twenty years old. Hannah is now eighteen and Jonathan fourteen! Even though this book has been primarily about loss, I want to assure you that God has, and continues to bring overwhelming joy to me in my life, and in the lives of my earthly children. In our homeschooling we have had so much fun together! Here are some things that have worked well for us:

We have made growing in our relationships with God, individually and as a family, our highest priority. We spent many hours learning how to hear the voice of God, both individually and as a family. We took risks, sharing what we thought God was saying to us. We also asked God to speak into our struggles and our pain. I have learned a lot along the way, but I can tell you that cultivating this prayer time together has been one of the best things we have done as a family! If you want to learn how to grow these prayer times in your life or as a family, I would love to help you. We also attended conferences, prayer events and weekly church services together. Keeping our focus on God, and nurturing all of our relationships, with Him and each other, has been our top priority.

We made time for reading together every day. We have read fascinating books that have taken us to different time periods and cultures. We have had so many interesting discussions while reading! Our favorite books are biographies. We loved learning about their childhood years. Then we enjoyed watching as each person's life unfolded, and how they stepped into God's plan for their lives! We always kept a story going, so when we were in those in-between moments we could get just one more chapter in!

We made time for ministry. We looked for ways we could reach out to others in the present. We didn't wait until Sara, Hannah and Jonathan grew up before they could have a ministry. We have taken meals to people in need, prayed for people, danced God's truth, and shared our faith in Christ at Walmart. It has been twenty years full of rich times of learning and growing. Twenty years of God daily downloading wisdom of what would work best for our family.

We made memories together. We have had many adventures together exploring caves, ocean shores and mountaintops. Our travels together have helped us work on our family relationships, and have also given us times to relax, laugh and make memories we will treasure forever.

We made time to try new things. Throughout their formative years, we have explored many different types of activities to draw out their interests and talents. They have tried dance, art, acting, and many different types of sports. Some of these things they loved and continued. Sara and Hannah love dance and art. Jonathan loves science, sports and music. We nurtured the talents and things they loved. But even the activities they didn't continue helped them grow.

When Sara was unsure about what career path to take for her college years, we sought out opportunities for her to shadow professionals in different career fields. For each experience we noted together what felt familiar, what was new, and what awakened something in her heart.

We were intentional about having fun and laughing. It is important to not only work together, but also to play together and have fun. Look for ways to bring laughter to your times together. Play games, do puzzles, spend time together outdoors.

As Sara and Hannah enter their college years, Jonathan and I will continue to enjoy the adventure of learning and listening to God. We look forward to seeing how God will lead us in the coming years.

As I look at this new generation of children, I see them growing up in a different culture than even my children have. It is important to know what challenges you are up against as a parent.

They live in such a unique time of history. They will never know a time without the Internet. They have always been able to ask Google any question they like.

These children will need to have their hearts awakened to the beauty of God and His creation. They will need help nurturing their capacities for waiting, silence and pondering.

With all the voices that are competing for their attention, we need to help them hear the voice of God, and discern His gentle leading in their lives.

Since we are all exposed to worldwide news and events, they will need help processing what they see and hear.

We will need to help them understand their uniqueness. We'll need to cultivate a sense of joy in fulfilling God's call on their lives, rather than living in competition.

They will need to understand their unique role in history, and that they are created by God for such a time as this.

They will need to know how to walk in a close relationship with God, and learn what it means to be a son or daughter of God!

Finally, use the following keys to help you parent in the light.

"This is the message we have heard from him and declare to you: God is light; in him there is no darkness at all." 1 John 1:5

Perspective is important. Keep eternity in mind each day, and treasure each moment God gives you. Work to make each moment the best it can be. Keep your FOCUS on the presence of God!

"Again Jesus spoke to them, saying, "I am the light of the world. Whoever follows me will not walk in darkness, but will have the light of life." John 8:12

Partner with others who can help you. Do you need ideas to help you connect more with your children? Are there obstacles that you need to overcome? Are you stuck in an area of your life? There is always hope. Listen for God to give you divine strategies for your family, and get help from a mentor or coach.

"I say, "Surely the darkness will hide me
and the light become night around me,"
even the darkness will not be dark to you;
the night will shine like the day,
for darkness is as light to you." Psalm 139:11-12

Pay attention to your heart, and find your passion. God gives us desires and dreams, and we need to pay attention to these longings. I have learned to become a student of my children, discovering where their gifts and talents lie, and then working hard to nurture and cultivate the treasure God has placed inside of them.
"But if we walk in the light, as he is in the light, we have fellowship with one another, and the blood of Jesus, his Son, purifies us from all sin." 1John 1:7

Your Path: Finally, keep moving on the right path with your eyes fixed on Jesus. You and your family are unique, since there will only be one of you in all history! That is why it is important not to compare, but to keep your focus. Let God's word be the light to your path.

"Your word is a lamp for my feet, a light on my path." Psalm 119:105

Thank you so much for reading my story! Before we move on to the final three chapters covering the armor of God, I would like to speak this blessing over you from Numbers 6:24-26:

May the Lord bless you and keep you,
May the Lord make his face shine on you
and be gracious to you;
the Lord turn his face toward you
and give you peace."

CHAPTER 13 THE ARMOR OF GOD

As I said previously, I believe understanding the armor of God is a key for living and parenting. That is why I am so excited to take a detailed look at the armor of God with you : last three chapters. I believe that each piece will help you walk in God's light, and in joy and peace as you fulfill the good works He has planned for you and your family!

Ephesians 2:10 says, *"For we are God's handiwork, created in Christ Jesus to do good works, which God prepared in advance for us to do."*

I also believe that the armor of God is a powerful tool for walking through loss with hope. So let's dig in together by first looking at the verses that surround the description of the armor in Ephesians Chapter Six.

The imagery used in this chapter is important. We are given armor because we are in a fierce battle. Read the following verses. As you read, notice how many times the word "stand" is repeated.

"Finally, be strong in the Lord and in his mighty power. Put on the full armor of God, so that you can take your stand against the devil's schemes. For our struggle is not against flesh and blood, but against the rulers, against the authorities, against the powers of this dark world and against the spiritual forces of evil in the heavenly realms. Therefore put on the full armor of God, so that when the day of evil comes, you may be able to stand your ground, and after you have done everything, to stand. Stand firm then, with the belt of truth buckled around your waist, with the breastplate of righteousness in place, and with your feet fitted with the readiness that comes from the gospel of

peace. In addition to all this, take up the shield of faith, with which you can extinguish all the flaming arrows of the evil one. Take the helmet of salvation and the sword of the Spirit, which is the word of God. And pray in the Spirit on all occasions with all kinds of prayers and requests. With this in mind, be alert and always keep on praying for all the Lord's people." Ephesians 6:10-18

How many times did you find the word "stand?"

In these eight verses the word "stand" is used four times! To stand means to be steadfast, referring to a person who is able to hold his or her position against the enemy. To stand means to persist, or to continue to persevere.[1]

The opposite of standing is someone who has fallen, or is sleeping or sitting. All of these positions point to inactivity, and being unaware, or to someone who is not effective. However, when a person is standing, he or she is ready, alert and useful.

God does not expect you to rely on your own strength or ability. God tells you to be strong in Him, and in His mighty power. He describes this power given to you just a few chapters earlier in the same book of Ephesians. In Ephesians Chapter One we read that God has given His incomparably great power to us who believe. Paul describes this power in verses 19b-23:

"That power is the same as the mighty strength He exerted when He raised Christ from the dead and seated Him at his right hand in the heavenly realms, far above all rule and authority, power and dominion, and every name that is invoked, not only in the present age but also in the one to come!"

God has given us everything we need to stand in the battle we find ourselves in. These gifts are not only for our protection, but they also enable us to stand firm!

As I have studied this passage, God revealed to me three things about each piece of armor that I had not seen before. Each piece is a gift we receive, a gift to grow in, and a gift to help us through times of loss.

Let me explain. Let's say your car breaks down, and you take it to a mechanic to get it fixed. Instead of getting your old worn out car back, the worker tells you that they have gifted you with a brand-new Toyota SUV at no charge. They hand you the keys and tell you to have a nice day. This is a gift that you did not pay for or earn. As a matter of fact, your car was not even a good trade-in because it was broken beyond repair! Once you have the keys in your hand you own the whole car! It is a complete gift given to you, that you have full access to right now!

However, at the same time it is a gift to grow in. Just being able to start the car and drive away does not mean that you have mastered all the features of the car you now own. Some of the amazing features will be discovered as you use the car, while others you may read about in the owner's manual. Either way, you will continue to learn all of the extras that came with your car that will make your ride more enjoyable. As you learn about and then use the features you find, your gift will become more valuable to you.

As you will see, each piece of the armor is a gift given to you that is complete and yours at the moment of reception. However, we will also look at how each piece of armor is at the same time a gift you can grow in.

To understand how the armor is a gift to help us through loss, let's go back to the car analogy. Recently I was driving and it started to snow. I turned on the windshield wipers and nothing happened. I was puzzled because they just worked the other day! I quickly took the next turn off the busy road and got onto a side street. I was able to make it home without the use of the windshield wipers, but I had to go slow. The wire from the wipers had become disconnected, so they no longer worked. I would like you to compare this disconnection to loss.

You have a working part, but it comes unhooked by trauma or loss, and now you need to restore the working part. We will look at how each one of these pieces of armor help us in this restoration.

Let's look together at each individual piece to understand what God had given us, how we can put on the armor by growing in each gift, and finally how each piece can help through times of loss.

The first piece mentioned in Ephesians 6 is the belt of truth.
"Stand firm then, with the belt of truth buckled around your waist,"
Eph. 6:14

The belt was a part of the armor that a soldier would put on first. The belt's job was to hold the rest of the armor in place.[2]

Let's look at how the belt of truth is a gift given to you. God is the source of all truth. God's word is truth! This gift is an important one because our enemy is the father of lies (John 8:44). Our enemy uses trickery, deceit and lies to lead us on a path of harm.

Imagine you are in front of two places to eat and you are hungry. You look at the two buildings and the choice appears to be easy. One building looks very nice, and there are a lot of people going in and out. In this building there are lights, music and good smells coming from the windows. The other building is small, you cannot see anyone inside, and you can't smell any food.

Even though the choice seems easy, you decide to look at each menu to learn the truth about each building before making your final decision. The attractive building has all the food that you like, and it makes the building look even better. Then you read the menu for the small restaurant. Inside you learn about the wonderful food and atmosphere that awaits you through the small door. Upon reading this information you also notice a review of the outwardly attractive building. What seems to be so good from an outside view is filled with unhealthy food that will make you sick!

God's word tells us the truth about God, about us, and about the world around us. The truth will always bring blessing to our lives and keep us from harm. We need to realize that the truth is our protection from things that look attractive on the outside, but will ultimately lead us on a path of death and destruction.

Our enemy does not want us to know all that God has given us as His child. He also doesn't want us to know the truth about the world. **We need to let God's Word be our guide, and not what looks pleasing to our eyes.**
God has given us the gift of truth in the person of Jesus Christ, and in His Word, the Bible, to lead us on the path of life. John 8:32 says, "Then you will know the truth, and the truth will set you free."

The belt of truth is a gift given for you to grow in as you learn to live a truthful life. If you take a picture of a scuba diver, you would

KAREN SUE SMITH

see his protective gear. In order to see the armor of a child of God, you would need to take a video.

Our armor can be seen as we live our lives, and can be heard in our words, and experienced in the fruit of our daily activities. We put on the belt of truth, and receive the gift of God's protection as we grow in living a truthful life. The more we know the truth and act on the truth, the more the belt of truth will be visible in our lives. This is how we grow in the gift of the belt of truth.

The belt of truth is also a gift given to you to help you through times of loss. When loss comes into our lives, circumstances speak messages to our hearts that are often like clouds that cover the truth. The belt of truth can keep us anchored to God in the midst of stormy skies. Meditate on the truth, and speak the truth in the midst of your loss. Let your foundation be that God never changes, and His words will always remain true.

~ 76 ~

CHAPTER 14 THE BREASTPLATE, THE FOOT GEAR, AND THE HELMET

The second piece of armor we find listed is the breastplate.

"with the breastplate of righteousness in place" Eph. 6:14

A soldier's breastplate was a big piece of armor. "The breastplate covered the soldier's body from his neck to his waist in the front and back." This gave the breastplate the ability to protect the soldier's heart, and all of his other major organs. "The breastplate was made of plated metal or chains, so that no sword or arrow could go through it."[1]

Let's look at how the breast plate of righteousness is a gift given to you. When we come to God and ask for his forgiveness, He gives us the righteousness of Christ. This piece of armor is especially dear to me as I remember how God allowed me to experience His righteousness covering me and surrounding me when Hudson was born.

Second Corinthians 5:21 says, *"God made him who had no sin to be sin for us, so that in him we might become the righteousness of God."*

Ephesians 1:7 says, *"In him (Jesus) we have redemption through his blood, the forgiveness of sins, in accordance with the riches of God's grace."*

God gives His righteousness to His children! This is an amazing gift that allows us to be forgiven, and be one hundred percent acceptable to God!

The purity that I experienced, the covering of God, remains etched in my heart! It is not about us and what we can do for God. It is about God giving us His righteousness as a gift.

Have you received this gift? If not, take a moment right now and pray this prayer: Lord Jesus, I need your righteousness. Thank you for dying on the cross for my sins. Thank you for doing for me what I could not do for myself. Thank you for taking my punishment, and giving me your righteousness and eternal life. Please forgive my sins and come into my life. Help me to know You, and to walk with You as my Savior and Lord. Amen.

If you prayed that prayer for the first time, I would love to know about it! Email me at lifeconnections35@gmail.com and I will help you with the next steps in your relationship with God.

The breastplate of righteousness is a gift given for you to grow in as you learn to live a pure life. Romans 8:3-4 says, "For what the law was powerless to do in that it was **weakened** by the sinful nature, God did by sending his own Son in the likeness of sinful man to be a sin offering. And so he condemned sin in sinful man, **in order that the righteous requirements of the law might be fully met in us,** who do not live according to the sinful nature but according to the Spirit."

Ephesians 4:22-24 reads, "*You were taught, with regard to your former way of life, to put off your old self, which is being corrupted by its deceitful desires; to be made new in the attitude of your minds; and to put on the **new self, created to be like God in true righteousness and holiness**.*"
Not only are you given the instant gift of Christ's righteousness, but as you depend on God He gives you the ability to live a

righteous life; a life that is different from the world; one that obeys God's Word and pleases God's heart.

You put on the breastplate of righteousness as you grow in living a righteous life, making decisions in light of God's purity.

The breastplate of righteousness is also a gift for times of loss. Maybe the loss you suffered exposed your weaknesses. If so, know that you are covered by the righteousness of Christ. Also, maybe healing from the loss will involve extending forgiveness to someone. Jesus paid for all your sins and the sins done against you when he died on the cross. With His last breath He said, "It is finished"(John 19:30). Our debt of sin had been paid!

The next piece of armor is the foot gear.

"with your feet fitted with the readiness that comes from the gospel of peace" Eph. 6:15

In Biblical times, soldiers wore heavy protective foot gear. The soles of the shoes were made so the soldier could have good footing in rough terrain, and so he would be steady in battle. The solder's footwear gave him the ability to move.[2]

Let's look at how the armor for your feet is a gift given to you. Because of what Jesus has done for us on the cross, we now have peace with God. What a solid foundation on which to walk, run, and fight!

Romans 5:1 says, *"Therefore, since we have been justified through faith, we have peace with God through our Lord Jesus Christ."*

KAREN SUE SMITH

In the book of Galatians, we learn that God has, through Christ, broken down barriers so that we can have peace in our relationships!

Galatians 3:28 reads, *"There is neither Jew nor Gentile, neither slave nor free, nor is there male and female, for you are all one in Christ Jesus."*

From these verses we learn that not only do we have peace with God, but Jesus has also given us a way to have peace with others.

The armor for your feet is a gift given for you to grow in as you learn to live a life of peace. Matthew 5:9 says, *"Blessed are the peacemakers, for they will be called children of God."*

Isaiah 52:7 says, *"How beautiful on the mountains are the feet of those who bring good news, who proclaim peace, who bring good tidings, who proclaim salvation, who say to Zion, "Your God reigns!"*

We put this piece of armor on as we grow in living a life of peace. Finding peace, especially in relationships may take time, work and wisdom, but the harvest reaped from these investments will be well worth your efforts. If you find any pieces of this armor hard to put on, ask for help. You are not alone in your struggles.

The armor for your feet is a gift in times of loss. Our enemy can deceive us, trick us, and hold us captive, but he cannot give us peace. Peace is a gift from God. Even if most of your life is in turmoil, ask God for peace, and then look for the area that He gives you this gift. For me, in my darkest hours God would grant me peace as I spent time with Him outdoors. Surrounded by the beauty of what He created, God poured peace into my heart. Still, one of my favorite things to do is hike, and talk to God as I walk. I love how God draws my heart to Him as I admire His handiwork all around me.

Look for where God is giving you peace in your life, and then follow that path.

"And your ears shall hear a word behind you, saying, "This is the way, walk in it," when you turn to the right or when you turn to the left." Isaiah 30:21

During times of loss there will be a temptation for your feet to take you to wrong places to find comfort apart from God. Yes, there can be comfort in wrong relationships, drugs or anything you use to numb the pain, but the problem is the numbing is only temporary. The short-lived pleasure or coping will only bring more pain to your troubled heart.

If you cannot find peace on your own, let others come alongside you to help you hear the voice of God, and experience His comfort.

The next piece of armor we will examine is the helmet.

"Take the helmet of salvation" Eph.6:17

The helmet was the part of the soldier's armor that protected his head. [3]

Let's look at how the helmet is a gift given to you. You are God's chosen child!

In Chapter One of Ephesians we read, *"For he (God) chose us in him before the creation of the world to be holy and blameless in his sight"* (Eph.1:4).

Being God's child is a gift. *"For it is by grace you have been saved, through faith—and this is not from yourselves, it is the gift of God - not by works, so that no one can boast"* (Eph. 2:8-9).

Being God's child is a gift that brings joy.

After Israel's King David committed the sins of adultery and murder (2 Samuel 11), He prayed for God to forgive him and create in him a clean heart. He also prayed that God would restore to him the joy of his salvation. Read his prayer below:

> *"Create in me a pure heart, O God,*
> *and renew a steadfast spirit within me.*
> *Do not cast me from your presence*
> *or take your Holy Spirit from me.*
> *Restore to me the joy of your salvation*
> *and grant me a willing spirit, to sustain me."*
> Psalm 51:10-12

There is a joy in our lives that flows naturally from salvation, because we are not only saved from sin, but we are now children of God!

The helmet of salvation is a gift given for you to grow in as you learn to live assured that you are a child of God. 1 John 5:12 says, "Whoever has the Son has life; whoever does not have the Son of God does not have life." When we have the Son we have life, and God wants you to grow in assurance of your salvation. Listen to what the following two verses say about assurance of salvation.

2 Peter 1:10-11 says, *"Therefore, my brothers and sisters, make every effort to confirm your calling and election. For if you do these things,*

you will never stumble, and you will receive a rich welcome into the eternal kingdom of our Lord and Savior Jesus Christ.

Romans 8:16 says, "*The Spirit himself testifies with our spirit that we are God's children.*"

God gives you eternal life, and then He assures you by His Holy Spirit that you are his own. Knowing that you belong to God allows you to walk with confidence.

The helmet of salvation provides increased protection as you grow in a life of assurance and confidence that you are God's son or daughter.

The Helmet of Salvation is a gift in times of loss. Our thoughts change the way our brains look! Carolyn Leaf talks about this idea in her book "Switch on Your Brain." She has actual brain photographs for thoughts that are in line with God's Word, and thoughts from the enemy. A thought that aligns with God's word looks like a healthy tree, while one that is contrary to the truth is dark. She writes, "our thoughts, imagination, and choices can change the structure and function of our brains on every level." [4] We need to pay attention to what thoughts we dwell on!

Loss gives a perfect opportunity to dwell on things that create darkness in our hearts and minds. Yes, we need to process our feelings, but what are the thoughts we are thinking about over and over again? Think of your brain like a hill where a fresh snow has just fallen. The first time sledding down the hill you are making a new path, so the way down is slower. However, each time you slide down, the path gets easier and faster. When you continue to think the same thoughts, you are actually creating a pathway in your brain that makes that line of thinking easier to think, and will eventually become etched in your brain.

Another important thing I learned in a sermon by Kris Vallotten is that our brains think using the least amount of energy. Think about a familiar route that you take every day. Ask yourself, is this the fastest route to get there or the shortest?
If you wanted the shortest route, you would have to go in a straight line, as the crow flies. So I guess you said the fastest route which included a road! Taking a road that is paved and maintained will get you to your destination much faster and easier! This is what your brain does. For example, say that you walk by someone and they do not say hello. Do you conclude "nobody likes me" because that is your usual way of thinking and a paved pathway? In contrast, the pathway to the thought, "he didn't see me, but I am important." is a longer, less trodden path. [5]

To put on the helmet of salvation means that the thoughts you think over and over are thoughts that show that: you are a child of God, and God loves you and has good plans for you; that you are important!

CHAPTER 15 THE SHIELD OF FAITH, THE SWORD OF THE SPIRIT, AND PRAYER

What do you need to make a batch of chocolate chip cookies? Besides all of the things that you would find at the grocery store, like flour, eggs and chocolate chips, you also need tools such as bowls, a spoon and an oven! The last two pieces of armor are more than just ingredients for your protection, they are tools that help you to advance in battle against your enemy.

Faith and the Word of God are tools given to you to make your life pleasing to the heart of God. These tools help you fulfill all that God has called you to do.

The gift of God's armor not only keeps you safe, but allows you to walk forward in freedom!

Let's take a closer look at the shield of faith.

"In addition to all this, take up the shield of faith, with which you can extinguish all the flaming arrows of the evil one." Eph. 6:16

A soldier's shield was about 2½ feet across and 4 feet long, so it offered double protection for almost every part of the soldier's body. The shield was made of wood, but was covered with cloth and thick leather, and then soaked in water. This ensured that any burning arrows which hit the shield would be extinguished rapidly. [1]

Let's look at how the shield of faith is a gift given to you. God is the source of all good gifts! God gives revelation and faith as a gift. In Matthew 16:17 Jesus replied to Peter, *"Blessed are you, Simon son of Jonah, for this was not revealed to you by flesh and blood, but by my Father in heaven."*

In 1 Corinthians 12:9 we learn that faith is one of the gifts of the Holy Spirit:

"to another faith by the same Spirit, to another gifts of healing by that one Spirit,"

Faith sees God's promises, even when circumstances give a different message. The eyes of faith see themselves and the world around them through the lens of God's Word.

The shield of faith is a gift given for you to grow in as you learn to live a life of faith. Faith is not only a gift given, but also a gift to grow in.

"So then faith comes by hearing, and hearing by the word of God." (Romans 10:17)

If you want to grow in the gift of faith, spend time in God's word! Memorize God's word. Sing God's word. Listen to God's word as you drive, or even as you go to sleep! Joshua 1:8 says:

"Keep this Book of the Law always on your lips; meditate on it day and night, so that you may be careful to do everything written in it. Then you will be prosperous and successful."

You can also follow the example of the apostles and pray that God will help your faith to grow. Luke 17:5 records their words, *"The apostles said to the Lord, "Increase our faith!""* We know that when we pray according to God's will that He hears our prayers and will answer.

1 John 5:14 says, "*This is the confidence we have in approaching God: that if we ask anything according to his will, he hears us.*"

The shield of faith is also a gift in times of loss. God gives you something because you need it! The shield of faith has a purpose, which is to extinguish all the flaming arrows of the evil one. Your enemy is not only a liar, but he is also your accuser.

Rev. 12:10 says, "*Then I heard a loud voice in heaven say: "Now have come the salvation and the power and the kingdom of our God, and the authority of his Messiah. For the accuser of our brothers and sisters, who accuses them before our God day and night, has been hurled down.*"

What you see and what you know to be true from God's Word may at times come into conflict. 2 Corinthians 5:7 says, "*For we live by faith, not by sight.*" Faith allows you to listen and obey God rather than believe the lies and accusations of the enemy and the world. This is especially important in times of loss. Pray that God will increase your faith. Look to God. He is your source of strength, grace, and faith.

The sixth piece of armor is the sword.

"*Take the helmet of salvation and the sword of the Spirit, which is the word of God.*" Eph. 6:17

A soldier carried a sword made of sharp steel into battle. [2]

The sword of the Spirit is a gift given to you. We are not left wondering what the sword of the Spirit is. We are told it is God's Word. There are two Greek words that refer to the Word of God. One is Logos, which refers to the written word of God, and the other is Rhema, which refers to a spoken word of God. A Rhema word is one that is specific to your situation, that God speaks to you. The Greek word used in this verse is Rhema. As you read the Bible, ask God to highlight the verse or verses that you are to fight with. God's Word is your sword, and is a gift given to sustain you and give you life each day.

The sword of the Spirit is a gift given for you to grow in as you learn to hear the voice of God. When God speaks to us, He will always speak in agreement with His written word. When you are discerning what God is speaking to you as you go forward in battle, test what you are hearing to see that it matches with the written Word of God. Ask God to confirm what He has spoken to you. When you have assurance that you have heard right, you have a powerful weapon to wield. Learning to hear God's voice takes practice. But growing in this ability is the key to walking forward in victory, and is well worth the effort!

The sword of the Spirit is also a gift in times of loss. When Jesus was tempted by Satan in the wilderness, he confronted the offers and words of Satan with the Word of God. Ask God to highlight to you what Scriptures He wants you to fight with. Let God's Word, which is living and active, bring life to you in the midst of your loss.

"For the word of God is alive and active. Sharper than any double-edged sword, it penetrates even to dividing soul and spirit, joints and marrow; it judges the thoughts and attitudes of the heart." Hebrews 4:12

You receive the gift of the sword of the Spirit as you live a life full of God's Word and according to God's Word.

The seventh weapon! Look at how this passage on spiritual armor in Ephesians concludes:

Ephesians 6:18 says, *"And pray in the Spirit on all occasions with all kinds of prayers and requests. With this in mind, be alert and always keep on praying for all the saints."*

The gift of prayer is given to you.

We read in Psalms 121:1-4:

> *"I lift up my eyes to the mountains*
> *where does my help come from?*
> *My help comes from the Lord,*
> *the Maker of heaven and earth.*
>
> *He will not let your foot slip*
> *he who watches over you will not slumber;*
> *indeed, he who watches over Israel*
> *will neither slumber nor sleep."*

God never slumbers or sleeps, and is always ready to hear our prayers! You receive the gift of God's protection as you live a life of prayer and constant connection with God.

Prayer is also a gift that you can grow in. Any relationship takes time to grow. Your relationship with God is no exception. Prayer is not just about talking to God, but also hearing His voice and spending time with Him. As you make this a regular habit you will come to know God more, and be more sensitive to His voice.

Be confident that God hears and answers prayer!

James 5:16-18 says, "The prayer of a righteous person is powerful and effective. Elijah was a human being, even as we are. He prayed earnestly that it would not rain, and it did not rain on the land for three and a half years. Again he prayed, and the heavens gave rain, and the earth produced its crops."

Prayer is also a gift in times of loss. Prayer has been the constant thread through all the times of loss we have walked through! I am so thankful for friends and family who have joined with us and prayed for us as we walked through the valley of the shadow of death!

I am reminded of the story in Exodus 17. Moses was praying and holding his hands up as the battle raged on. But then he got weary and could not hold his hands up in prayer any longer. Then the Israelites began to lose the battle. Aaron and Hur came to help Moses. As they stood beside him and helped him hold up his hands in prayer, the Israelites were victorious!

Putting all the pieces of the armor together. Every piece of the armor is important! As we have seen, putting on God's armor is more than just saying a morning prayer. Putting on God's armor is a way of life. It is not a formula to follow, but growing in your relationship with the living God, and seeing each piece of armor become part of your lifestyle.

If someone followed you around for a week with a video camera, would they see God's armor in your actions and words? Would they write down truth, righteousness, peace, faith, assurance, and a listening and prayerful heart as characteristics of your life?

Growing ourselves and helping our children grow in each one of these areas is so important, and it will allow you to live in hope and freedom. The goal of the armor is to stay connected to God. He wants you to know Him, and to walk with Him.

God gives you all these gifts so you and your children can stand and not fall!

As I conclude this section and this book, I want to leave you **focusing** on God, the One who can and will sustain you! I love the final verses in Jude, which read, "*To Him who is able to keep you from falling and present you before his glorious presence without fault and with great joy--to the only God our Savior be glory, majesty, power and authority, through Jesus Christ our Lord, before all ages, now and forevermore! Amen.*" Jude 1:24-25

CONCLUSION

Thank you again for taking time to read my book.

I love teaching, coaching and mentoring. No matter what your educational choice, I would love to help you find the right path for you and your children. There are answers when you are stuck; there is peace you can find in the midst of conflict. There are wonderful things to explore and experience along the way - things that you will enjoy just as much, or maybe even more than your children!

Together we will find the next right step for you! Visit my website to sign up for your FREE strategy session.

Do you want to know how to help your children stay connected to God and you as they grow up in a culture where they are always connected to the Internet? You can find information on my website about my online course, "Raising Connected Kids."

Finally, on my website you can also sign up for free resources to help you grow in your relationship with God. I have produced a thanksgiving journal sheet and four short videos. These resources will help you create space in your life to spend time with God. Each video comes with a journal sheet to fill out as you talk to God.

To sign up for your FREE session and access the above resources, visit my website at www.lifeconnectionsacademy.com.

If you enjoyed reading my story, I would love for you to leave a book review on Amazon!

I would also love to hear from you!

If you have any comments or questions, email me at <u>lifeconnections35@gmail.com</u>

AUTHOR'S PAGE

Karen Sue Smith, author, speaker, life coach and home educator, loves helping families grow in their connections to God and each other.

She graduated from Taylor University with a Bachelor of Arts degree in Psychology. She then enjoyed serving on the staff of Campus Crusade for Christ for five years. Her love for God's Word continued to increase as she earned her Master of Divinity Degree from Gordon Conwell Theological Seminary in South Hamilton, Massachusetts.

During her nineteen years of homeschooling, she has written Sunday School curriculums, and served in several different children's ministry positions.

Throughout her homeschooling years, she has searched for keys that would aid children's spiritual growth. Her favorite training has been her certification in the Catechesis of the Good Shepherd Levels I and II. She also participated in training for Godly Play, and Precept Children's Ministry. She put this training into practice by developing and leading a "Time With God Group" for twelve years, giving space and time for children to develop their relationships with God.

She has also acquired training to help children overcome educational challenges. She has completed the Brain Gym training and is a certified Structure of Intelligence examiner. Her oldest daughter is in college, but she is still enjoying the journey of home educating her other two children. She lives in Wheaton, Illinois with her husband and three children.

APPENDIX A

Jessie's Book

Jessie Smith
In utero May 2002-August 1, 2002

On June 9, 2002, before a full morning of yard sales, we took the pregnancy test. Our hearts were filled with joy, as we learned that you, baby Jessie, had entered our lives. Soon, all our family and friends knew about you! As we told them, we asked them to pray for us and for you!

Although your life on earth was short, each day you were with us was precious to us. The following are memories that we will always cherish.

We will always remember that your life was filled with celebrations.

We prepared and planned for your Dad's 35th birthday on June 20th.

Hannah turned two on July 15th.

We had a lot of fun shopping, cooking and creating as we decorated and anticipated both parties.

We celebrated life as we thanked God for the gift of each other, and the blessings that He daily pours through us to each other.

We will always remember that your life was filled with prayer.

Your dad and I prayed for you often, individually and together. We prayed for you at breakfast, at lunch, and at dinner. I often asked Sara to pray when we sat down to eat lunch together. Her usual reply was, "It is too hard-you pray."

I will always treasure the July day during your life with us when I asked Sara to pray and she said, "Yes!" She prayed a beautiful prayer, thanking God for the day and praying for you. When she finished praying, Hannah also wanted to pray for the very first time! She said, "Dear Jesus, Mom, Dad, Sara, New Baby, Amen."

During your life we made a special effort to surround you with worship and prayer. During a time of prayer, God reminded me of His love for me, and reminded me to bring all the concerns of my heart to Him. He also assured me that you were in the river of Jesus's love.

We will always remember that your life was filled with times of joy.

It was during your life that Hannah discovered the overpasses on the freeway. She called them tunnels. We all, but especially Hannah, anticipated each "tunnel," and laughed and shouted as we passed through each one.

We spent a lot of time at playgrounds, swinging, sliding, playing and enjoying the fresh ocean breeze.

Whether we were shopping, playing or watching a video, you were a part of our times of joy and happiness.

We will always remember that your life was filled with a mother's love.

Even before I took the pregnancy test, somehow I knew that you had entered my life. I felt happy and full of life.
You made me hungry for pizza, for veggie hot dogs, and fried eggs on toast.

Every night as I would go to sleep, I would pray for you, and pleasantly dream about the day when I would hold you in my arms and see your sweet face.

We will always remember that your life was filled with a father's love.

Dwight writes, "You often filled my thoughts and prayers, especially as I traveled to and from Boston. As with Sara and Hannah, from the beginning I always prayed for your total well-being, both physically and spiritually - that you would be blessed all the days of your life.

During your life my focus was on reading about the greatness of God and His sovereignty. God was at work building in my life a new hunger and thirst for His righteousness. Our heart's cry was strengthened to see the glory and greatness of God's name proclaimed.

Each day I gladly sacrificed for you. I often did extra work around the house so your mom could rest. I took Sara and Hannah shopping, or to the playground to give your mom even more times to rest. I spent myself each day in a way to shower love, provision, and care upon your life.

Precious Jessie, you were and are a wanted baby. You will always be in our hearts. We thank God for your life, and for sharing you with us, even though only for a short time.

We look forward to the day when we will be able to see you and rejoice together in the presence of our Lord and Savior Jesus Christ." Love, Dad, Mom, Sara and Hannah.

APPENDIX B

How do you write a memory book for a baby that you were only able to cherish for a few weeks? Ask yourself, were there any special events that you attended during this time?

Was there a song that meant a lot to you?

What verses from the Bible stood out to you, or are currently speaking to you now?

Name your baby, then tell the story of why you picked that particular name.

Write a love note to your baby.

In my book for Arron, I included an explanation of the Bible passage when the angel told Mary she would be the Mother of Jesus. This explanation really helped me see the significance of Arron's life.

Arron's Book

Arron Smith
In utero July-August 30, 2008

A form of Aaron, which means "shining light."

"that you may be blameless and innocent, children of God without blemish in the midst of a crooked and twisted generation, among whom you shine as lights in the world," Philippians 2:14

In Luke 1:34-43 we read about Mary saying yes to be the mother of God's Son, Jesus. "Although we do not know the exact time frame of these verses, we know that it was a very short period from the time that Jesus was conceived in Mary's womb, and when she visited Elizabeth. Some say it was just a few days traveling. "In other words when Elizabeth was filled with the Holy Spirit and prophesied upon Mary's arrival-the child in your womb is the Lord" Mary was only a matter of days into her pregnancy." (Hayford, 30)

This passage opened my eyes to the significance of life from the moment of conception!

Read the following passage with these thoughts in mind.

Luke 1:34-43 says:

""How will this be," Mary asked the angel, "since I am a virgin?"

The angel answered, "The Holy Spirit will come on you, and the power of the Most High will overshadow you. So the holy one to be born will be called the Son of God. Even Elizabeth your relative is going to have a child in her old age, and she who was said to be unable to conceive is in her sixth month. For no word from God will ever fail."

"I am the Lord's servant," Mary answered. "May your word to me be fulfilled." Then the angel left her.

At that time Mary got ready and hurried to a town in the hill country of Judea, where she entered Zechariah's home and greeted Elizabeth. When Elizabeth heard Mary's greeting, the baby leaped in her womb, and Elizabeth was filled with the Holy Spirit.

In a loud voice she exclaimed: "Blessed are you among women, and blessed is the child you will bear! But why am I so favored, that *the mother of my Lord* should come to me? As soon as the sound of your greeting reached my ears, the baby in my womb leaped for joy. Blessed is she who has believed that the Lord would fulfill his promises to her!'"

"From the moment of conception, the child is a real, valid and meaningful person." (Hayford)

"Your eyes saw my unformed body; all the days ordained for me were written in your book before one of them came to be." Psalm 139:16

We are fearfully and wonderfully made, knit by God in our mother's womb!

"In the third week after conception the lobes of the brain are distinguishable. In the fourth week, the head and face are recognizable and the heart starts to beat. During weeks five and six the eyes are identifiable and legs are putting on flesh and muscle. In the eighth week, the embryo moves to the fetal stage, and during the following weeks sex can be identified and the baby can begin to turn its head, squint, frown, make a fist and even get the hiccups. All of this is before the end of the first three months in the womb!" (Hayford)

These are the passages of Scripture that spoke to me during your life, and after you went to heaven.

"The Lord is my shepherd, I lack nothing. He makes me lie down in green pastures, he leads me beside quiet waters, he refreshes my soul. He guides me along the right paths for his name's sake. Even though I walk through the darkest valley, I will fear no evil, for you are with me; your rod and your staff, they comfort me. You prepare a table before me in the presence of my enemies. You anoint my head with oil; my cup overflows. Surely your goodness and love will follow me all the days of my life, and I will dwell in the house of the Lord forever." Psalm 23

"Do you not know? Have you not heard? The Lord is the everlasting God, the Creator of the ends of the earth. He will not grow tired or weary, and his understanding no one can fathom. He gives strength to the weary and increases the power of the weak. Even youths grow tired and weary, and young men stumble and fall; but those who hope in the Lord will renew their strength. They will soar on wings like eagles; they will run and not grow weary, they will walk and not be faint." Isaiah 40:28-31

"Brothers and sisters, we do not want you to be uninformed about those who sleep in death, so that you do not grieve like the rest of mankind, who have no hope. For we believe that Jesus died and rose again, and so we believe that God will bring with Jesus those who have fallen asleep in him. According to the Lord's word, we tell you that we who are still alive, who are left until the coming of the Lord, will certainly not precede those who have fallen asleep. For the Lord himself will come down from heaven, with a loud command, with the voice of the archangel and with the trumpet call of God, and the dead in Christ will rise first. After that, we who are still alive and are left will be caught up together with them in the clouds to meet the Lord in the air. And so we will be with the Lord forever. Therefore encourage one another with these words." 1 Thessalonians 4:13-18

Arron, even though your life here on earth with us was only for a brief time, we thank God for you and look forward to seeing you one day. You are and will always be a treasured part of our family. Love, Dad, Mom, Sara, Hannah and Jonathan.

NOTES

Chapter 5
1 Sittser, Gerald Lawson. *A Grace Disguised: How the Soul Grows through Loss.* Zondervan, 2006. p.17
2 Ibid. p.51.
3 Ibid. p.42

Chapter 6
1
https://www.google.com/search?rlz=1C5CHFA_enUS815US815&q=Bill+Johnson+quotes

Chapter 8
1 Gaebelein, Frank E., et al. The Expositor's Bible Commentary: Ephesians through Philemon. Zondervan Pub. House, 1990, p320.
2 Piper, John. *Future Grace: The Purifying Power of the Promises of God.* Multnomah Books, 2012. p.28.

Chapter 10
1 Hogue, Rodney Hogue, "Healing." Life Church St. Charles, 4 March. 2017

Chapter 13
1 Jones, Timothy P. The Armor of God. Rose Publishing, 2013.
2 Ibid.

Chapter 14
1 Jones, Timothy P. The Armor of God. Rose Publishing, 2013.
2 Ibid.
3 Ibid.
4 Leaf, Caroline. *Switch on Your Brain: The Key to Peak Happiness, Thinking, and Health.* Baker Books, 2013 p.20,21,68
5 Vallotton, Kris. "Learning to Think." Bethel Podcast. Bethel Podcast, 2 Dec. 2018.

Chapter 15
1 Jones, Timothy P. The Armor of God. Rose Publishing, 2013.
2 Ibid.

BIBLIOGRAPHY

Addison, Doug. On-line Prophetic Activation School. "Hearing The Voice Of God 365."

Gaebelein, Frank E., et al. The Expositor's Bible Commentary: Ephesians through Philemon. Zondervan Pub. House, 1990.

Hayford, Jack W. *I'll Hold You in Heaven*. Chosen, 2015.

Hogue, Rodney Hogue, "Healing." Life Church St. Charles, 4 March. 2017.

Jones, Timothy P. The Armor of God. Rose Publishing, 2013.

Leaf, Caroline. *Switch on Your Brain: The Key to Peak Happiness, Thinking, and Health*. Baker Books, 2013.

Murphy, Edward F. *The Handbook for Spiritual Warfare*. T. Nelson, 1992.

Piper, John. *Future Grace: The Purifying Power of the Promises of God*. Multnomah Books, 2012.

Sittser, Gerald Lawson. *A Grace Disguised: How the Soul Grows through Loss*. Zondervan, 2006.

THAYER, JOSEPH. *THAYER'S GREEK-ENGLISH LEXICON OF THE NEW TESTAMENT: Coded with the Numbering System from ... Strong's Exhaustive Concordance of the Bible.* PMAPUBLISHING COM, 2017.

Vallotton, Kris. "Learning to Think." Bethel Podcast. Bethel Podcast, 2 Dec. 2018.

Virkler, Mark. *Dialogue with God:* Peacemakers Ministries, 1986.

37251875R00063

Made in the USA
Lexington, KY
26 April 2019